Video Games

TECHNOLOGY 360

Video Games

KEVIN HILE

LUCENT BOOKS
A part of Gale, Cengage Learning

GALE
CENGAGE Learning™

Detroit • New York • San Francisco • New Haven, Conn • Waterville, Maine • London

© 2010 Gale, Cengage Learning

LIBRARY OF CONGRESS CATALOGING-IN-PUBLICATION DATA

Hile, Kevin.
  Video games / by Kevin Hile.
      p. cm. -- (Technology 360)
  Includes bibliographical references and index.
  ISBN 978-1-4205-0170-4 (hardcover)
  1. Video games--Social aspects. 2. Video games--History. I. Title.
  GV1469.34.S52H55 2009
  794.8--dc22
                                    2009006250

Lucent Books
27500 Drake Rd
Farmington Hills MI 48331

ISBN-13: 978-1-4205-0170-4
ISBN-10: 1-4205-0170-4

Printed in the United States of America
2 3 4 5 6 7 13 12 11 10

Printed by Bang Printing, Brainerd, MN, 2nd Ptg., 08/2010

CONTENTS

FOREWORD

"As we go forward, I hope we're going to continue to use technology to make really big differences in how people live and work."—Sergey Brin, co-founder of Google.

The past few decades have seen some amazing advances in technology. Many of these changes have had a direct and measureable impact on the way people live, work, and play. Communication tools, such as cell phones, satellites, and the Internet, allow people to keep in constant contact across longer distances and from the most remote places. In fields related to medicine, existing technologies— digital imaging devices, robotics and lasers, for example—are being used to redefine surgical procedures and diagnostic techniques. As technology has become more complex, however, so have the related ethical, legal, and safety issues.

Psychologist B.F. Skinner once noted that "the real problem is not whether machines think but whether men do." Recent advances in technology have, in many cases, drastically changed the way people view the world around them. They can have a conversation with someone across the globe at lightning speed, access a huge universe of information with the click of a key, or become an avatar in a virtual world of their own making. While advances like these have been viewed as a great boon in some quarters, they have also opened the door to questions about whether or not the speed of technological advancement has come at an unspoken price. A closer examination of the evolution and use of these devices provides a deeper understanding of the social, cultural, and ethical implications that they may hold for our future.

Technology 360 not only explores how evolving technologies work, but also examines the short- and long-term impact of their use on society as a whole. Each volume in Technology 360 focuses on a particular invention, device or family of similar devices, exploring how the device was developed; how it works; its impact on society; and possible future uses. Volumes also contain a timeline specific to each topic, a glossary of technical terms used in the text, and a subject index. Sidebars, photos and detailed illustrations, tables, charts, and graphs help further illuminate the text.

Titles in this series emphasize inventions and devices familiar to most readers, such as robotics, digital cameras, iPods, and video games. Not only will users get an easy-to-understand, "nuts and bolts" overview of these inventions, they will also learn just how much these devices have evolved. For example, in 1973 a Motorola cell phone weighed about 2 pounds (.907kg) and cost $4000.00—today, cell phones weigh only a few ounces and are inexpensive enough for every member of the family to have one. Lasers—long a staple of the industrial world—have become highly effective surgical tools, capable of reshaping the cornea of the eye and cleaning clogged arteries. Early video games were played on large machines in arcades; now, many families play games on sophisticated home systems that allow for multiple players and cross-location networking.

IMPORTANT DATES

1952
A.S. Douglas invents the first computer game. It is a Tic-Tac-Toe game pitting the player against the computer.

1958
The first video game, *Tennis for Two*, which used an oscilloscope to display the tennis ball and net, is created.

1962
The first video game for a regular computer monitor, *Spacewar*, is developed.

1967
Ralph H. Baer creates the first video game system: the Odyssey.

1972
Nolan Bushnell founds Atari, the first big video game company. *Pong* debuts as an arcade game.

1979
Mattel Electronics debuts Intellivision, a home system that combined gaming with computing capabilities.

1982
The Commodore 64 debuts. It is a combination of video game player and home computer.

1950   **1960**   **1970**   **1980**

1977
The Atari 2600 system is released and becomes the first popular 8-bit processor game console.

1980
Pac-Man debuts.

1983-1985
The video arcade business declines in popularity. *Super Mario Brothers* debuts in 1985 and is credited for revitalizing the video game industry.

in the Development of Video Games

1989
The most successful handheld game console to date, Nintendo's Game Boy, is released.

2003
Linden Labs creates the online life simulation game *Second Life,* an online MMORPG.

2006
Nintendo releases the Wii system, with its unique Wiimote that senses the hand motions of players.

1995
The PlayStation from Sony is released.

1993-1994
Congressional hearings on violent video games results in the establishment of The Entertainment Software Rating Board (ESRB), to ensure that video games are labeled with age appropriateness levels and content descriptions.

2007
The Xbox is enhanced as the Xbox 360 Elite video game system. It includes a cable port and 120 gigabytes of hard drive memory.

1990   **2000**   **2010**

1992
Mortal Kombat debuts, spurring on a debate about violence in video games.

1993
Doom is released by id Software. It becomes the most successful first-person shooter game of the 1990s. *Myst* is released and becomes the most popular puzzle game of its type.

2000
The Sims debuts on CD-ROM and is later released online.

Bringing Games to Life and Life to Our Games

People have always played games. The ancient Chinese, for example, played a game called mehen (meaning "snake") that combined a board game with moves of pieces shaped like lions, dogs, and balls on a large field. The Egyptians loved the game senet—a board game resembling cribbage in some ways. Over the centuries, games have slowly changed, with many popular ones, such as chess and checkers, still being played today. There are card games; board games; word games, like crossword puzzles; and math games, like Sudoku.

With the onset of the technological revolution in electronics in the 1970s and 1980s, and the rise of computers, games changed in a fundamental way. No longer were people moving pieces on a board by hand or writing out answers on a piece of paper. Instead they began playing games using a computer monitor. They began experiencing games in a virtual—rather than physical—world.

This advance seemed innocent enough at first. While the technology was still new, the primitive and limited capabilities of early video games were more of a novelty than a cultural phenomenon. The first people to play video games were engineers and other highly educated technophiles, people enthusiastic about technology who not only understood

how to play computerized games but who could also write the programming for them. Later crude games like *Pong,* *Asteroids,* and *Donkey Kong* had limited graphics capabilities. Many players lost interest in them by the early 1980s.

Technology progressed, however, and video games became more and more realistic. Today video and the ability to control characters' actions on the screen have become so convincingly true-to-life that the experience is almost like living in another world. Whether using a home system, such as the Nintendo Wii or PlayStation 3, or playing online, players are now submerged in a virtual reality where they can assume another character's identity, seek outlandish adventures in another world, make friends, communicate with

Games have been played throughout history. Ancient Egyptians, for example, played the game of senet, a board game resembling cribbage.

other players, and even conduct real business transactions or attend business seminars.

Video games have come a long way, and they have become more than just an entertaining pastime; in 2008 they were a $35-billion industry worldwide. They have become part of our culture and an influential part of our lives. Many people have embraced the video game revolution as a benefit to society, making a case for how it has increased social networking, but others worry that it encourages violence, laziness, and social isolation.

The future holds many possibilities for video games, including branching out beyond gaming and evolving into a kind of second reality where people can socialize, conduct business, and even go to school. How we use them will be up to us.

CHAPTER 1

Transformation of the Arcade

Like many other technological inventions, the sophisticated video games of the twenty-first century can be traced back to much more primitive, simple roots. The forerunner of today's popular video games was the pinball machine. Although not the refined, computerized pinball machines we see today, the first modern pinball machines appeared in the 1930s. They evolved from a nineteenth-century game called bagatelle that was similar to Skee-Ball. This was modified into a game called Baffle Ball—invented by David Gottlieb in 1931. Baffle Ball was more similar to pinball games and included the bumpers and flippers with which anyone who has played pinball is familiar. Gottlieb, as well as a growing number of competitors, made money by placing pinball machines in penny arcades. They then collected the change that players inserted into the games, giving the arcade owners a cut of the money.

It might surprise people today that, in the first half of the twentieth century, pinball machines were illegal. This was because slot machine manufacturers decided to take advantage of pinball's popularity. They combined the features of slots and pinball into new games that combined skill and luck. Because gambling was illegal in some states like New York, it was banned for many decades. To get around this issue,

In the early 1900s pinball machines were illegal because they were considered a gambling game and gambling was illegal in many parts of the United States.

designers modified pinball games to make sure that they involved more skill than luck. Although still running into some legal issues, pinball makers became increasingly successful. By the 1950s, pinball machines could be found in arcades and diners all across America. They were extremely popular with kids and teenagers.

By the 1950s and early 1960s, new advances in electronics were enhancing the pinball experience, but they also were offering hints of a new industry that would largely replace the old staple of pinball gaming.

The First Computer Games

The first computer game was a version of tic-tac-toe that was created in 1952 by A.S. Douglas, a Cambridge University doctoral student who wrote the program as part of his PhD dissertation (a final, long paper that all doctoral candidates need to complete to earn their degrees) on the interaction between people and computers. Then in the early 1960s, advancements in computer technology made it possible for computer games to emerge as an amusement for nonscientists. Originally programmers communicated with computers using punch cards and reading the results of calculations on printouts from teletype machines. Computer monitors came into use in the 1960s. At the time, however, they were only available at universities.

While university computers were primarily used for research, someone came along and decided to write a program, called *Spacewar,* for fun. The creator of this game is a matter of some debate. Some say that Brookhaven National Laboratory scientist Willy Higinbotham invented it. Higinbotham was the creator of the game *Tennis for Two,* which he invented in 1958.

An electronic oscilloscope, shown here, was used to display the first video game Tennis for Two.

It was played on an analog computer with an oscilloscope display at the Brookhaven National Laboratory. Others credit Steve Russell, a student at the Massachusetts Institute of Technology (MIT), for creating *Spacewar* in 1962.

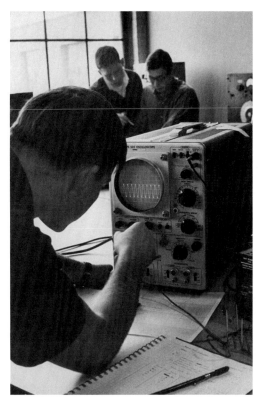

Russell was a member of MIT's Tech Model Railroad Club (TMRC). While members enjoyed building model railroads, they were also among the first computer users to start pushing the limits of what computers were originally intended to do, which was fast mathematical calculations. "These strange college students, with their funny jargon and nerdy ways, did more to start the computer revolution than any Silicon Valley [California] engineering team," says Steven L. Kent, a lifelong video game player and electronic entertainment columnist. Kent also says,

Naturally curious, these MIT students had devoted their lives to intellectual tinkering. They believed in a cooperative society and imagined themselves living in a utopian world in which people shared information— sometimes without regard to property rights. Once they discovered computers, they became known as "hackers." Before that, they were simply nerds.[1]

Russell, according to Kent, modified a previously written program (these programs were stored on ticker tapes in desk drawers that were easily accessed) to create *Spacewar*, the first interactive computer game, with help from some of his friends. The simple game involved two spaceships trying to outmaneuver and destroy each other. The two ships were controlled by four switches, which operated rotation, thrust, and missile firing. *Spacewar* was designed to be played on a programmable data processor-1 (PDP-1). The PDP-1 was a $120,000 computer with a 15-inch (38cm) video display.

The PDP-1 allowed *Spacewar* to be played by two players, but it was not long before players saw the need for remote controllers. Kent explains,

> *Spacewar* was originally controlled by toggle switches built into a panel on the computer. But the awkwardly placed switches gave the players sore elbows, and after a while some TMRC members cobbled together another set of switches and ran wires between them and the PDP-1—the world's first controllers for the world's first video game.[2]

Games for the Television

The next important development for video games came in 1967, when Ralph H. Baer came up with the idea of inventing computer games that could be played on a television set. Baer was a manager leading a team of engineers at Sanders Associates, a defense contractor. Working with television manufacturer Magnavox, Baer created Odyssey, the first game system. Odyssey only contained some transistors and diodes that, when connected by a cable to a television, could produce simple dots and other basic graphics. But that was about all they could do. Author Lisa Ennis explains, "The Odyssey connected to a regular television antenna terminal and was hardwired with twelve games, all variations of Ping-Pong. There was no sound or color, and each of the games required a different plastic overlay for the television screen."[3]

No microprocessor technology was used at all for memory purposes, which meant that neither games nor player statistics could be saved. When Odyssey was turned off and then turned on again, players started a game from the beginning.

Because Sanders Associates was going through some financial difficulties and because the company did not really wish to go into the game industry,

Inside an Early Video Game

Early television video games used transistor-to-transistor logic (TTL) and programs such as FORTRAN. TTL involved a circuit board and was a standard form of circuit communication used in mainframe computers, while FORTRAN was an early mathematical program language invented back in the 1950s (modern-day game programmers use more sophisticated languages such as C++). These tools allowed game programmers to create simple graphics that moved across a screen and could interact with each other (such as a paddle hitting a ball), but they were very limited by today's standards.

Baer's Odyssey system was marketed only for a short time in the early 1970s. The idea of a computer tennis game, like the one hardwired into the Odyssey, would soon be copied by the company Atari. Atari was led by electrical engineer and company founder, Nolan Bushnell, and his partner, Ted Dabney.

Bushnell, a fan of *Spacewar* when he was a college student, worked at video game arcades during the summers when he was not at school. He gained experience repairing pinball machines. He decided to make a coin-operated version of the game that could be played in arcades. This resulted in the 1971 debut of the game *Computer Space*.

While only about 3,000 games of *Computer Space* sold, Bushnell founded Atari the next year. Then Bushnell hired Al Alcorn with the hope of developing *Computer Space* into a television game. To get Alcorn started, Bushnell asked him to create a paddleball game. The young Alcorn created a game that, while similar to Baer's original tennis game, was not only considerably more advanced but also used cheaper components. Alcorn added sound, allowed the "ball" to bounce off walls, and added ball acceleration capabilities that made the game much more fun.

In 1972 Atari released Alcorn's game with the name *Pong*, a variation of Ping-Pong, which was very similar to Baer's Odyssey tennis game. First appearing in arcades, and then as a home version in 1975, *Pong* was a huge hit. It sold tens of thousands of games.

Some Impacts of *Pong*

Nolan Bushnell founded Atari in 1972 and soon thereafter released the iconic video game Pong.

The early popularity of *Pong* in the mid-1970s had a couple of impacts. The release of the game resulted in the first legal battle between two computer game companies: Magnavox and Atari. Baer, unlike Steve Russell, had the foresight to patent his game. So, when Magnavox sued Atari in 1973 for creating and selling *Pong*, the case was settled out of court.

How *Pong* Got Sound

For those people who have ever played Atari's *Pong,* one feature of the game remains very memorable: the distinctive "boop! boop! be-doop!" sound of the ball hitting paddles and eventually scoring. This sound was added to the game by programmer Al Alcorn in desperation. His bosses wanted him to create a "boop" sound or the sound of a cheering or booing audience. But mimicking such noises was beyond what Alcorn knew how to do at the time and it seemed beyond the capabilities of the hardware he was using. Instead, he investigated what computer technology he had available. A sync generator, a circuit that helps synchronize events occurring in the computer, created a signal that could be pirated to generate the "boop" sound, so Alcorn simply used it. For something that was just slapped together in half a day's worth of programming, Alcorn created a sound that was both charming and memorable.

Baer and Magnavox received seven hundred thousand dollars from Atari. From then on, royalties had to be paid to Magnavox for the right to sell *Pong.* This would just be the first of many future legal battles between established and emerging video game companies.

Another impact of *Pong* and other video games would be more far-reaching. In an interview, Bushnell said he felt that early video games introduced average people to the possibilities of computers in the home. He also said,

> Up until the video games, people didn't really think of being able to control a video image. It's kind of like training wheels. There are a lot of processes that go along in starting up the video game, playing the video game, closing it down, scoring, various things. There are processes that are very similar to what you have to do to run a personal computer. And some of the technology that we had to connect a television set and a video game were actually used in the Apple II [computer].[4]

So, games such as *Pong* actually got people thinking that home computing could be possible and fun. This interest in computers and games was encouraged with the invention of Intellivision by Mattel Electronics. Intellivision, which debuted in 1979 for just seven hundred dollars, could be used to play video games, but it also came with a keyboard and could be used like a personal home computer.

Pong was also important in that it marked a big advance in computer technology. The home version of *Pong* (originally named *Home Pong*) was different from the Magnavox tennis game. It had a computer chip inside the console—instead of wiring—that was developed by Alcorn, Harold Lee, and Bob Brown at Atari. The new chip resulted in sharper graphics and allowed players to play using only one controller instead of two. When *Home Pong* was released in 1974, "the chip in [it] was the highest performance-integrated circuit ever used in a consumer product."[5]

The success of *Pong* inspired copycats such as Coleco, a company that originally made leather craft kits (*Coleco* stands for Connecticut Leather Company) and plastics. It went into the video game business in 1975 and came out with a tennis game console called Telestar. Then, an innovative company called Fairchild Camera and Instruments created the first game cartridges. Originally, as with the Odyssey and *Pong* consoles, the technology was hardwired into the system. This meant that people could only play the games already in the system. With game cartridges, people could buy new games, plug them into the console and switch games back and forth. The first console designed by Fairchild was the Channel-F Video Entertainment System.

The Rise of Video Arcade Games

After *Pong,* Atari put out variations of the original game, such as *Breakout,* a game in which players used paddles to hit a ball that then knocked out blocks on the screen. The company also began to create more innovative games, such as *Steeple Chase* (a horse-racing game) and *Stunt Cycle* (bus-jumping stunts on a motorcycle). Copycat companies emerged and created their own games, too.

Video arcades had what could be called the first violent video games. These included *Maneater,* a game based on the successful 1975 horror movie *Jaws,* which was about a man-eating shark, and *Gunfight,* a cowboy shoot-'em-up game. *Gunfight* was an important game because it was the first video arcade

game with a microprocessor inside, rather than wiring. This advance allowed for more detail in the game, including more graphical obstacles between the gunfighters. This made the game more challenging and interesting for players.

What motivated video game manufacturers to improve technology was fierce market competition. Atari had the upper hand at first, but rival businesses emerged, introducing game innovations, such as *Tank,* a popular video game created by Steve Bristow of Kee Games. *Sea Wolf,* a battling submarine game produced by the company Midway, was also a hit. Players even got to use a periscope, pretending to be a World War II sea commander.

Early video games were often two-person shooting or racing games, or hitting-the-ball games. A game called *Death Race,* introduced by Exidy Games, was also hugely popular. It involved racing a car and scoring points for running over pedestrians. This created a controversy that led the developers to change the people to demons. Kent says, "Exidy spokespersons claimed that *Death Race* was about running over demons and had nothing to do with killing people. In

Racing games were popular during the evolution of early video arcade games.

private they agreed that the scandal had boosted their sales. When *Death Race II* arrived in 1977, it had the same basic theme—running over stick figures."[6]

Violence in video games would not become an industry-wide controversy, though, until the 1980s and 1990s. Such concerns fell by the wayside as a new generation of video arcade games started a full-fledged craze.

A Profitable Craze

Like the hula-hoop craze in the 1950s, video arcade games would enjoy their own golden era. "Video game arcades sprang up in shopping malls and small, 'corner arcades' appeared in restaurants, grocery stores, bars and movie theaters all over the United States and other countries during the late 1970s and early 1980s," notes a writer on the gaming Web site Wager Web. "Games such as *Space Invaders* (1978), *Galaxian* (1979), *Pac-Man* (1980), *Battlezone* (1980), and *Donkey Kong* (1981) were especially popular."[7] Other classics of the era include *Centipede, Space Invaders, Missile Command,* and the race-car game *Pole Position.*

Donkey Kong Gets Its Name

Donkey Kong is a classic video game about a big gorilla who steals a plumber's girlfriend and fends off rescue by throwing big barrels at her boyfriend. It was created by Nintendo programmer Shigeru Miyamoto. Originally he called the game Stubborn Gorilla, but that did not seem very catchy. He changed *stubborn* to *donkey,* as in stubborn mule and added "Kong" after the famous movie gorilla King Kong.

This choice caused some trouble for Nintendo, however, when Universal Studios sued Nintendo for copyright infringement. In 1982 a judge ruled that Universal did not actually own the rights to the King Kong franchise because the studio itself had proven the character of Kong was no longer copyrighted in a previous legal action when Universal wanted to make a remake of the movie that RKO Pictures had originally filmed. *Donkey Kong* survived the lawsuit and is still a popular game today for those who enjoy the classics.

Pac-Man, a game in which a simple, round, yellow character gobbles up objects in a maze and is chased by ghosts, was a complete sensation. According to Western Illinois professor and journalist Bill Knight, "*Pac-Man* sold more than 350,000 arcade units in the 1980's, dethroning leading games of the era, such as *Space Invaders* and *Asteroids*."[8] *Pac-Man* even inspired a Saturday morning cartoon series, as well as lots of merchandise.

From 1978 through 1983, video arcade games were hugely popular. Game manufacturers raked in the cash. An arcade game like *Space Invaders,* for example, cost an arcade shop owner about seventeen hundred dollars to purchase in 1978, which was a big investment at that time. However, a popular game such as this "earned between $300 and $400 a week,"[9] according to Kent, so the store owner would quickly recover the purchase price and then some.

In the early 1980s, Pac-Man *was the most popular video arcade game.*

The video arcade business spawned new companies that created hardware, software, or both. Atari was still the software leader at the time, but others were getting into the act, as well. For example, in 1978 Cinematronics released the game *Asteroids*, which became successful. Meanwhile, coin-operated games were popular in Japan, and a businessman named Masaya Nakamura founded the Namco company in his homeland to take advantage of this demand. And, American companies like Atari and Sega were shipping video games to Japan.

To promote its games Atari held a national arcade game tournament in New York, New York, in October 1981 and a

Inside Video Game Consoles

Video game consoles and arcade games are like minicomputers. However, unlike a home personal computer or Apple computer, they were originally designed only to play games. Other than this limitation, they are very similar to home computers.

Arcade games have microprocessors with imprinted circuit boards containing hundreds of microchips that store the game programs. An arcade game has two computers in the game case: One controls the game motion and the other operates the sound. Home and handheld systems have only one central processing unit (CPU). Buttons and/or joysticks serve as input devices to the CPU. The CPU processes this input from the controls, checks them with the read only memory (ROM) that contains the game information and then sends the results to the display (arcade screen, television screen, or handheld LCD display.) A temporary memory card (random access memory, or RAM) is used to interpret player moves, keep score, and keep track of other ongoing information during an active game. When the game is over, the RAM data is not stored, unless the player saves the game. There is no automatic backup system, like on a home computer.

Recent upgrades now allow people to use video game consoles to perform tasks similar to computers such as play movies or surf the Internet.

championship in Chicago, Illinois, the same month. While the Chicago tournament only drew about 250 players (versus between 10,000 and 15,000 estimated at the New York City tournament), the idea of competitive gaming was formed and would later evolve into a full-time profession for some people.

Another offshoot of the video arcade game was the entertainment restaurant. Atari's Nolan Bushnell founded Chuck E. Cheese as a way to attract new customers to his company's video games. The pizza restaurant features animatronic animals playing music, costumed characters, and video and other arcade games. The target audience is children, who, of course, are accompanied by their parents. Video games then became a form of entertainment that involved the entire family and not just game-loving kids.

There was a problem with all this success, however. So many new companies popped up, many of them making inferior, poor-performing games, that the market was flooded with games by 1983. Consumers were turned off by the poor–quality games, and the industry crashed that year. Companies like Coleco and Mattel exited the video game business, and even giants like Atari struggled. Although the video game business went into decline, Chuck E. Cheese managed to survive.

Technological Advancements

Video games had a marked influence on American business. New companies and new industries were created to meet the demand for new and better games. Even more important was the industry's influence in spurring the advancement of computer technology. When computers were invented as a way to speed up mathematical calculations, it was enough to interact with a computer through punch cards and dot-matrix paper printouts. Such input-output relationships are not very interesting for playing games, however. Games demand visual interaction, interesting graphics, high-speed microprocessors, and easy-to-operate control pads or joysticks.

Video game manufacturers understood this. They provided constant pressure to create better and better microprocessors within consoles for television games. In 1977 Atari came out with the Atari 2600, which was the first popular 8-bit processor game console. Atari continued over several years to advance its console, coming out with the 5200 in 1982, the 7800 in 1986, the Lynx (for handheld games) in 1989, and the Jaguar in 1993.

Video game joysticks, like this one, were used to spur the advancement of home computer games.

Eight-bit processors were inevitably replaced with 16-bit processors, which could make calculations twice as fast and increase reaction time on the screen. Advances in microprocessors helped spur on the development of home computers,

Handheld Games

Game developers came up with a way to make video games portable in 1976, when Mattel came out with *Auto Race*. The game had very limited graphics projected on an LCD display, and an underpowered microprocessor limited the game's abilities. Racing cars represented by dashes moved jerkily across the screen. Despite such limitations, handheld games grew in popularity, which meant that people could spend even more time playing games than they did before. Various sports games were released, as well as stripped-down versions of arcade games like *Donkey Kong* and *Space Invaders*. The popular Game Boy was released in 1989, the same time as the Atari Lynx, but the Lynx was more expensive, so most customers purchased a Game Boy. Players liked the Game Boy and the Lynx because they were easy to use and game cartridges were inexpensive to buy.

The next big advance was color handhelds, such as Game Boy Color and Word Swan Color, which were released in the late 1990s. The technology was combined with MP3 players and personal digital assistants (PDAs) in the N-Gage and Tapwave Zodiac, and in 2004, the Nintendo DS added touch-screen capabilities. The DS and PlayStation Portable also included Wi-Fi Internet connectivity so players could easily download new games.

such as the Apple II (1977) and the Commodore 64 (1982). These computers, while usable for basic word processing and spreadsheet tasks, were often used for playing games in the home. As microprocessors improved and became smaller, they made handheld games possible and had applications to portable communications devices, such as cellular phones.

From 1988 to 1990 gaming systems with advanced microprocessors, such as the Sega Genesis, sped up game play. CD-ROM-driven games were introduced in the early 1990s. This led to the possibility of three-dimensional graphics games, such as 1993's *Star Fox*, which was played on the Super Nintendo system. "The importance of the switch to CD-based software can't be stressed enough," notes game historian Jason Weesner. "Prior to the advent of the CD as a medium for game development, games were limited in scope by the size of the cartridge they came on."[10] At the time, game cartridges held one or two megabytes of memory, while game CDs held 640 megabytes.

Improved graphics, quicker processing speeds, and controller advances also had impacts on other industries. For example, joysticks, originally used by pilots to control real aircraft in the early twentieth century, were improved thanks to gaming. Computer gaming helped advance joystick responsiveness, which led to practical uses in industry (such as operating cranes, excavators, assembly line equipment), science (such as controlling deep-sea robots), and aiding the handicapped (as controls on motorized wheelchairs). Combining joysticks with vivid graphics made simulators much more realistic, too, not just for gaming, but also for military training.

The amazing advances video games made during the 1970s and 1980s created an entire new industry. Although arcade games fell into disfavor in the mid-1980s, other areas, such as handheld and home games, found a following. Games played on personal computers (PCs) and Apple computers using CDs, DVDs, and the Internet gained popularity in the 1990s and beyond. All of this would have an impact not only on technology but also on society overall.

BITS & BYTES

640 megabytes

Amount of memory a CD-ROM game can store

CHAPTER 2

Video Games and Violence

Many of the early video games, such as *Pong, Mario Brothers,* and *Pac-Man,* were pretty innocent in nature. The action in such games is distinctly rated G. Even *Spacewar* and *Asteroids* only had ships shooting little white dots at each other. As games became more advanced and realistic, however, the violence in them became more of a concern to parents because of the increasingly frequent emphasis on killing opponents in graphically gruesome ways.

One of the first controversial games was *Death Race* (1976), which had players running over people with cars. Even though the victims did not look realistic—they were just stick figures—the controversy stirred enough concern that the television news program *60 Minutes* aired a story about it.

Martial Arts Arcade Games

The debate about whether or not video games inspire violent behavior became more heated with the rise of martial arts arcade games in the 1980s. Although video games originated in the United States, their wild popularity in Japan inspired the creation of new companies in Asia. Japanese game

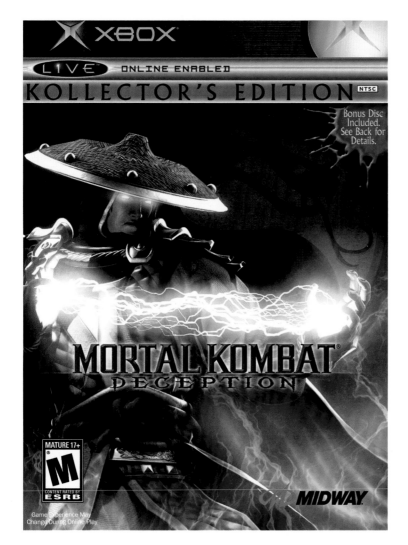

Mortal Kombat, *though very popular with gamers, was criticized by others for its realistic depiction of violence and death.*

designer Yoshiki Okamoto created combat games, like *Time Pilot* and *1942*, in the 1980s. These games did reasonably well, but Okamoto was running out of ideas for new games. He was getting desperate that he might lose his job at Capcom in Osaka, Japan. Then, he was inspired by a game called *Double Dragon II: The Revenge*.

The game had rather unsophisticated graphics and the action between the players (gang members fighting each other), was clunky at best. Okamoto proposed to his company that the game could be greatly improved. The result was 1989's *Final Fight*. This game was one of the first to have characters that looked more like real people. Not only that, but they had very individual looks. For example, one fighter looked like the real-life professional wrestler Andre the Giant. Okamoto also developed ways for players to act out a variety of kung fu moves using variations of only two controls: attack and jump.

Final Fight was a bestselling game and would lead to the 1991 release of the enhanced *Street Fighter II: The World Warrior* (an improved version of a 1987 game). *Final Fight* also made martial arts games popular, which would lead to the most controversial game of its day, *Mortal Kombat*.

Mortal Kombat began as an arcade video game in 1992 (home versions and sequels would later appear). Created by programmers Ed Boon and John Tobias, *Mortal Kombat* features human martial arts experts who find themselves transported to another dimension. There, they serve as representatives of Earth and have to fight monstrous opponents to the death in a martial arts tournament. If they lose, Earth is doomed.

Critics of the game objected to the blood and gore. It was particularly disturbing because the characters looked so real. The graphics were based on photographs that had been digitally animated. Fighters in the game won if they took down their opponent three times. On the third fall, the winner performed a "fatality" move. These were extra-grisly actions. "Fatalities ranged from Kano [one of the characters] wrenching his opponents' hearts out of their chests to Scorpion [another character] pulling out their spines and skulls,"[11] says Steven L. Kent, a lifelong video game player and electronic entertainment columnist.

Mortal Kombat was a megahit in the arcades. The appeal was the gut-wrenching action. As Jeff Greeson, editor in chief of the Realm of Mortal Kombat Web site, says, "*Mortal Kombat* not only stood out, it grabbed you by the shirt collar and demanded your attention. *Mortal Kombat* had the biggest and most realistic characters ever featured in a video game at the time. You were literally watching digitally animated photographs of people flying through the air and beating the living hell out of each other."[12]

In their book, *Grand Theft Childhood*, authors Lawrence Kutner and Cheryl K. Olson, the husband and wife team who founded the Harvard Medical School Center for Mental Health and Media, discuss interviews that they conducted with kids who enjoyed *Mortal Kombat*. They were seeking to understand the appeal of the violent game. One youngster named Joe explained that he liked the fatality moves the best because "they made the graphics good. It's not realistic; it's like, fancy and fun."[13] Kutner and Olson remark, "Some researchers have distinguished emotions that are related to admiration and artistry (aesthetic emotions) from feelings related to experiences in the game world (representative emotions) or even in the real world."[14]

In other words, young people playing *Mortal Kombat* easily understood this violence was not real and that it was not even the point. They actually enjoyed and admired the quality of the programming and graphics that made the game so cool.

First-Person Shooters

At the same time that *Mortal Kombat* was enjoying a great following, a new generation of game designers started creating violent games for personal home computers and game systems. Personal computer (PC) and TV console games still had some catching up to do with arcade games in the early 1990s. Graphics, for the most part, still looked like groups of colored pixels, or dots, and were not very lifelike. And games still had no scrolling capabilities.

In arcades scrolling had become the norm in games such as *Super Mario Brothers 3*. Programmer John Carmack was responsible for one of the greatest advances in home gaming. Working for a new company called id Software, founded by John Romero, Carmack created a new computer engine that is "the program code that controls such things as the speed, scrolling, game flow, graphics quality, and operating system compatibility of a game."[15]

VISUAL EVOLUTION OF GAME CONTROLLERS

1 Early Switch Controls. *Example: Magnavox Odyssey 100*

2 Joysticks. *Example: Atari 2600, Atari 5200*

3 A two button controller is introduced with start and pause options and a "D-Pad," designed to champion the joystick. *Example: NES controller*

4 More buttons are added to support increasingly complex games, especially fighting games like *Street Fighter*. Controllers become more curved to better fit in players' hands. *Example: Sega Genesis*

5 Shoulder buttons are added. *Examples: SNES controller and Playstation controller*

6 For better control in 3D games, the analog stick was added; similar to a trigger on a gun a "Z" trigger may be placed under the controller, making first-person shooter games more natural. *Example: N64 controller*

7 Popularity of the analog stick gives rise to dual analog controllers. *Example: Playstation Duel Shock*

8 Dreamcast controller offers a unique Visual Memory Unit, a screen that allows players to see extra game information. *Example: Dreamcast controller*

9 Rumble packs become the standard and analog sticks become touch sensitive, allowing the player to press down on the stick to perform a different move. *Examples: PS2, X-box, GameCubes*

10 Controllers become wireless. *Example: XBOX 360 controller*

11 With the addition of accelerometer and gyroscope technology, Nintendo's Wii remote offers increased ability to operate in 3D space. Moving the controller allows players to shift their view in the game. *Example: Nintendo Wii remote and nunchuck*

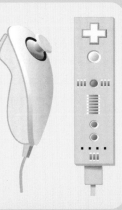

Id released its first game, *Commander Keen,* in 1991. "*Commander Keen* was a platform game, that is, a 2-dimensional game in which the player's character would jump around on platforms, avoiding obstacles like enemies and spikes," according to OldDoom.com moderator Jake Gilbert. "*Commander Keen* sold very well. This is because of id's revolutionary smooth scrolling technique. It actually wasn't really revolutionary, id just figured out how to do what Nintendo could."[16]

The next year, id released *Wolfenstein 3-D,* the original first-person shooter. The game was an upgrade of a much older game—1981's *Castle Wolfenstein*—which was a maze game in which the player tries to escape a Nazi castle with secret war plans. *Wolfenstein 3-D* was also set in a German, World War II–era castle. This time, the goal is to shoot as many Nazis as possible and simply escape the castle.

Wolfenstein 3-D, *the original first-person shooter home video game, was released in 1992 by id Software. Pictured is id's founder, John Romero.*

Like *Mortal Kombat, Wolfenstein 3-D* drew attention for its shock value because it showed the slain Nazis falling down and dying in pools of blood. Romero, however, argued that the reason the game was so popular "was the super-fast 3D rendering engine and movement. Most of the raves came from the pure adrenaline rush of speeding at 70 frames per second through corridors and mowing down Nazis."[17]

The Rating Game

In an effort to prevent young people from playing games that are too violent, the U.S. Congress pressured software developers to set up a rating system similar to the one used for movies. Congressional hearings were held in 1993, mostly in reaction to games such as *Mortal Kombat* and *Night Trap.* Released in1992, *Night Trap* originally played off of VHS tapes but was later adapted to Sega systems and for PCs.

Video Game Ratings

The Entertainment Software Rating Board, which was founded in 1994 as part of the nonprofit Entertainment Software Association, uses the following ratings to ensure that video games are labeled with age appropriateness levels and content descriptions:

- **C (childhood):** Suitable for children three years of age and older; contains nothing offensive.

- **E (everyone):** Suitable for children ages six and older; may contain some mild language or violence.

- **E 10+ (everyone 10+):** Suitable for children ages 10 and older; may contain more mild language or violence, as well as suggestive themes.

- **T (teen):** Suitable for ages 13 and older; may contain mild violence (possibly including blood), suggestive themes, some strong language or crude humor, and possibly simulated gambling.

- **M (mature):** Suitable for ages 17 and older; may include strong images of violence, strong language, and sexual content.

- **AO (adults only):** For ages 18 and older only; may include long graphic scenes of violence, nudity, and sex.

- **RP (rating pending):** Not yet rated.

Entertainment Software Rating Board, www.esrb.org/ratings/ratings_guide.jsp.

The plot involves a player entering a house inhabited by vampires and trying to find and rescue a woman inside.

Politicians had heard stories that *Night Trap* involved murdering women in gory fashion. Kent reports, however, that "reading the transcripts of the 1993 hearings, it is hard to believe that anybody had ever actually played *Night Trap*. Few people bothered to acknowledge that the goal of *Night Trap* was not to kill women but to save them from vampires."[18] Ironically it was the congressional hearings that gave *Night Trap* a lot of free publicity. Without all the publicity, the video game probably would not have sold as well as it did.

The result of the hearings, which lasted until early 1994, was that industry leaders, such as Sega, Atari, Electronic Arts, Nintendo, and 3DO, got together and worked out a rating system. They also created the Interactive Digital Software Association to serve as a lobbying group in Washington, D.C., and the independent Entertainment Software Rating Board (ESRB). The ESRB would fairly rate games according to how age appropriate they were.

Doom and *Quake* Shake Things Up

In 1993 id Software released *Doom*. The game marked a huge advance in computer gaming graphics in terms of realistic, three-dimensional pictures. There was very little point to *Doom* and its sequels, *Doom 2* and *Doom 3,* other than killing ugly monsters from hell while wandering through a seemingly endless maze. Certain upgrades were made with each version. There were more weapons, different monsters and music, and the graphics became increasingly—even stunningly—realistic, but it was essentially the same game.

Doom became almost an obsession for many game players across the United States, as well as other countries. One reason for this was Romero's enlightened idea to offer the game as shareware on the Internet. This meant people could download a sample of the

> ## BITS & BYTES
>
> **77 percent**
> The amount that violent crimes committed by juveniles decreased from 1993 (the year *Doom* was released) to 2003

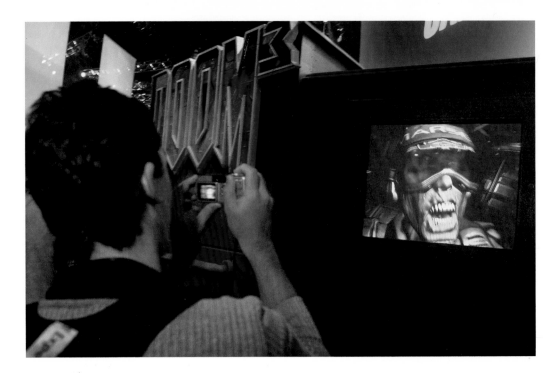

Doom marked a huge advance in computer gaming graphics in terms of realistic, three-dimensional pictures.

game onto their home (and, often, business) computer and try it out for free. Once tempted by *Doom*'s graphics and violent game play, most people purchased the complete version. "*Doom* . . . brought attention to shareware, validating it as a viable means of software delivery and establishing the idea of free demonstration copies as a marketing method,"[19] says Kent.

Doom would also come in home console versions for such systems as the Nintendo PlayStation, which would also be the case for other first-person shooters. *Quake* debuted in 1996 and continued id Software's tradition of improving graphics and sound with every new release. While *Doom* had enemy characters and settings that, despite the three-dimensional maze effects, looked flat, *Quake* made the three-dimensional concept come to life. Characters appeared to be three-dimensional because players could view them from different angles, and players could move around walls and other objects, as well, and they appeared as they did in real life. Texture and lighting effects were also greatly improved. The *Quake 3: Arena* version, released in 1999, allowed for team play, as well.

Parents, teachers, and psychologists were shocked by the level of violence displayed in *Doom* and *Quake.* The games seemed designed only to provide the experience of what it was like to kill other human beings. The controversy came to a head in 1999 when the violence turned all too real.

Columbine Massacre

On April 20, 1999, the quiet town of Columbine, Colorado, was rocked by an explosively violent shooting that shocked the world. Two students, Dylan Klebold (age seventeen) and Eric Harris (age eighteen), entered Columbine High School armed with explosives and high-powered guns. They killed a dozen classmates and a teacher before turning the guns on themselves and committing suicide. Investigators later learned that both teenagers were obsessed with the shooter games *Mortal Kombat, Doom,* and *Duke Nukem,* an early 1990s game from Apogee Software.

The families of the victims blamed video game companies for encouraging Klebold and Harris's actions. In 2001 the families sued twenty-five companies, including Sega, Nintendo, AOL Time Warner, and id Software, for a total of $5 billion in damages. The lawsuit was later dismissed, with the judge stating that Klebold and Harris were the sole guilty parties of the crime.

The wounds of Columbine were reopened in 2005, when game designer Danny Ledonne released *Super Columbine Massacre* RPG (RPG means "role-playing game"). The game has players taking on the role of Harris and then Klebold. The teens wander around the school killing students and faculty with semiautomatic weapons. "In the end, players learn there's really

While the Super Columbine Massacre RPG *video game angered many people,* Columbine shooting survivor Richard Castaldo, pictured, *found himself drawn to the game.*

no way to win,"[20] writes journalist Jose Antonio Vargas in a *Washington Post* newspaper article.

While the game angered many people—especially survivors, family, and friends of the victims—at least one victim, Richard Castaldo, was fascinated. Castaldo was shot in the back at Columbine and is now paralyzed from the waist down. Still, he says, "It's weird for me to say this, I guess, but there's something about it that I appreciated, seeing the game from the killers' perspective."[21]

Ledonne says that his purpose for creating *Super Columbine Massacre* RPG was to show the insanity of what Harris and Klebold did. "If you make it far enough in the game, you see very graphic photos of Eric and Dylan lying dead. . . . I can't think of a more effective way to confront their actions and the consequences those actions had."[22] Ledonne is among those who feel that video games have the potential to send a positive message to players.

Violence with a Plot

Two of the most controversial games in recent years are *Grand Theft Auto* (first released in 1997 by BMG Interactive Entertainment) and *Halo* (first released in 2001 by Bungie Studios, followed by *Halo 2* in 2004 and *Halo 3* in 2007), both of which have become series with many variations to play. *Grand Theft Auto* has a gritty, urban setting in which players assume the role of a leading criminal within an organized syndicate. One of the innovations of games like *Grand Theft Auto* is that players can play the game without a goal and simply do whatever they want within the game's setting, including committing crimes like stealing cars or killing people. This type of video is called a sandbox game, a name which comes from the idea that you can make all sorts of things out of the game in the same way that you can make all sorts of things out of sand in a sandbox.

Halo 1 is a science-fiction video game from Microsoft Game Studios that was premiered with the Xbox game system in 2001. The scenario involves a war in the twenty-sixth century that is being waged between humans and aliens who are trying to dominate Earth. The humans are cybernetically engineered supersoldiers who have help from an artificial intelligence called Cortana. A first-person shooter game, *Halo,* for which sandbox modes are also available, is mostly about shooting and blowing up aliens and their machines.

Grand Theft Auto, and its various versions, revolve around violence, committing crimes, and killing people.

In 2005 the families of two slain police officers filed a lawsuit against the makers of *Grand Theft Auto.* In 2003 Devin Moore, who was reportedly driving a stolen car, shot and killed officers James Crump and Arnold Strickland when he was cornered in Fayette, Alabama. The families of the officers claimed that the sixteen-year-old Moore had been inspired to commit his crime by his love of the games *Grand Theft Auto III* and *Grand Theft Auto: Vice City.* They blamed not only Sony for making the games, but also Wal-Mart and GameStop for selling the rated-M games to the

The Female Image in Video Games

Critics of video games not only target the violence they portray but also the way they portray women. Many games, they point out, show women as sexual objects who are dressed provocatively. Even worse, in games such as *Grand Theft Auto,* they are shown as prostitutes who are physically attacked by male characters. One particularly objectionable video game, according to some critics, is *BMX XXX,* a 2002 game that features scantily clad women doing tricks on BMX bicycles.

Many action games—because they are designed for young men—continue to have female characters who are young, sexy, and scantily dressed. However, as the game industry begins to realize that they have many women customers, this is starting to change. Women in the *Sims,* for example, look much more like realistic people than Lara Croft in *Tomb Raider.*

underage Moore. Moore was convicted of murder in 2005, but the judge in the trial refused to allow evidence about how *Grand Theft Auto* might have affected Moore's behavior in the incident.

As was the case with *Mortal Kombat,* some gaming authorities maintain that players realize that the violence and plot in *Grand Theft Auto* is silly and unrealistic. Therefore, people are not about to commit murder just because they saw it in a game. Journalist Rashawn Blanchard writes, "The level of absurdity that is seen in these games is something that gamers know they can't do in real life—that is one of the core reasons that many people play the game."[23]

Investigating Violent Games and Aggression

Since the 1990s, video game companies have observed that their most popular games tend to be the ones that are more violent. An article in a 2001 issue of the journal *Psychological Science* notes, "Numerous educational, nonviolent strategy, and sports games exist, but the most heavily marketed and consumed games are violent ones. Fourth-grade girls (59%)

and boys (73%) report that the majority of their favorite games are violent
ones."[24]

The authors of the article, psychology
professors Craig A. Anderson and Brad
J. Bushman of Iowa State University,
conducted experiments in which they
measured the reactions of game players and how the games affected their
behavior. They concluded that the
"results clearly support the hypothesis
that exposure to violent video games
poses a public-health threat to children and youths, including college-age
individuals."[25] Anderson and Bushman
studied over four thousand game players (about half over the age of eighteen and half younger than eighteen).
They found that players tended to act
more aggressively and also think more
aggressive thoughts at the end of the
experiment than at the beginning.

In 2000, Doug Lowenstein, president of the Interactive Digital Software Association, claimed that studies proved no link between violent video games and aggressive behavior amongst those who play them. Other studies, however, have claimed that there is a link.

Leaders in the video game industry deny that their violent games have negative effects on players. In a television
interview for *World News Today* in 2000, the president of the
Interactive Digital Software Association, Doug Lowenstein,
stated: "I think the issue has been vastly overblown and over-
stated, often by politicians and others who don't fully understand, frankly, this industry. There is absolutely no evidence,
none, that playing a violent video game leads to aggressive
behavior."[26]

Studies over the last few years by psychologists and other
scientists have agreed with Lowenstein's position. Some
experts have said that there is no strong link between violence
and video games. According to Patrick Kierkegaard, a PhD
candidate at the School of Computer Science and Electronic
Engineering at the University of Essex in England, early studies on violent games were biased. In other words, scientists
had negative opinions about violent video games and that
they designed their experiments to support their ideas.

According to Kierkegaard, "violent crime, particularly among the young, has decreased dramatically since the early 1990s." There were 1.36 million violent crimes in the United States in 2005 versus 1.42 million in 2004, "while video games have steadily increased in popularity and use."[27]

Another expert who supports the idea that violent games may not cause people to be violent is Massachusetts Institute of Technology professor Henry Jenkins. In an article on the PBS Web site, Jenkins states,

> most . . . studies are inconclusive and many have been criticized on methodological grounds. In these studies, media images are removed from any narrative context. Subjects are asked to engage with content that they would not normally consume and may not understand. Finally, the laboratory context is radically different from the environments where games would normally be played. Most studies found a correlation, not a causal relationship, which means the research could simply show that aggressive people like aggressive entertainment.[28]

Concerns about violent video games remain, however, and the concern is not just about the psychological effects of violence. Many worry, too, about obsessive behavior in players who allow video games to take over their lives. Players who become addicted to video games may not commit crimes, but their obsession can cause other problems with their physical and mental health.

CHAPTER 3

Minds and Bodies at Risk?

Violence in video games has received a lot of media attention, especially since the 1990s. Parents of children who love violent video games have been especially concerned about their children's emotional health. But there are several other issues of concern.

One worry is that children and teens who play violent video games obsessively will become socially isolated and not form healthy social bonds—friendships—with people their own age or develop the skills necessary to communicate with others. This may make their lives as adults more difficult. For instance, they may fail to learn how to behave in a business setting, or socializing or dating may be awkward because they have not developed the social skills necessary to interact with other people.

Because playing video games has for the most part been a sedentary activity during which snacking and sipping sodas is common, parents have long worried that hours spent sitting in front of a TV or computer monitor could lead to diabetes and other health problems.

In a 2007 Harris Interactive survey of 1,178 children and teenagers who played video games, boys eighteen and younger played video games sixteen to eighteen hours a week, while girls played eight to ten hours on average. The researchers who designed the survey concluded that "playing video games is related to several important negative outcomes for youth, including poorer school performance, increased physical aggression, and increased risk of . . . obesity."[29]

The children and teens who participated in the survey said, however, that the content of the video games did not affect their behavior. Also, only 46 percent of those surveyed said their parents limited the number of hours they played and 56 percent said their parents would not let them play certain games.

Selling to an Audience

Because many people think that children and teenagers are more likely to be influenced by video games than adults, psychologists and other experts have focused on how games affect young people. Game developers, however, consider young men between the ages of eighteen and thirty-four to be their biggest customers. Marketing studies have shown that these players spend the most amount of money on video games.

Since video game companies feel that older players are more likely to become customers, they focus on producing more games that are rated for mature audiences. But kids under sixteen also like to play these M-rated games. By law, they are not allowed to purchase them themselves, so they convince their parents or other relatives to buy them, or they play them online or at a friend's home. According to a study published in a 2007 *Journal of Adolescent Health* of 1,126 seventh and eight graders who played video games regularly, nearly half played at least one violent game regularly and of those children, two-thirds were boys and the rest were girls. When it comes to adult players, the audience for video games may be changing. An article on the Web site Online Media Daily reported in 2007: "Of the more than 1,000 respondents to the Denizens of Digitivity survey . . . 44% of women said they own a gaming console such as a Wii, Xbox or PlayStation, compared with just 39% of men."[30]

Although it seems that women players are not avid gamers like men, they are playing video games more and more, and they tend to like the less-violent ones, such as the music game *Guitar Hero* and *Dance Dance Revolution,* which actually involves a lot of physical activity as players match dance steps to lighted squares on a stage. Video game manufacturers are aware of the trend, and the result has been more variety in the types of games available. According to one research result, "nearly twice as many boys as girls (39 percent versus 20 percent) preferred games with a story, and girls were more apt than boys to prefer games with no story (25 percent versus 14 percent)."[31]

Some studies show that women enjoy playing puzzle games, such as *Sudoku,* and they prefer games that do not have scantily clad, buxom females and lots of senseless shooting. This does not mean they do not enjoy other types of games, though. Phaedra Boinodiris, chief executive officer of WomenGamers.com, an Internet gaming site for female gamers, says, "the only difference [between male and female

Michigan governor Jennifer Granholm signed legislation in 2005 making it illegal to sell or rent adult-rated video games to those ages 17 and younger.

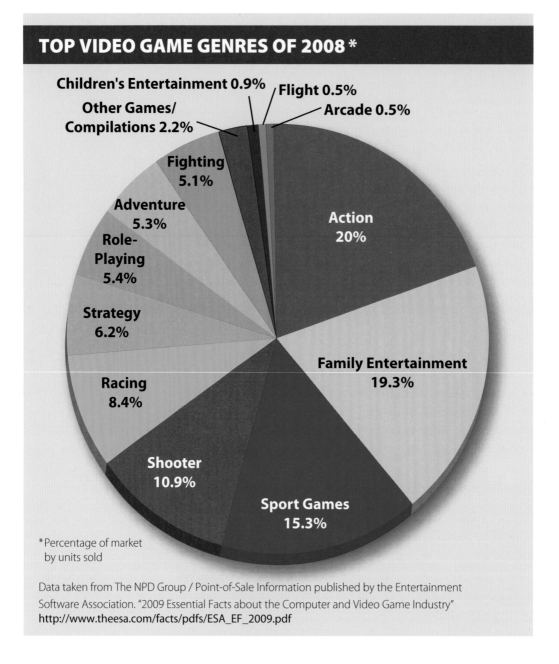

TOP VIDEO GAME GENRES OF 2008 *

Children's Entertainment 0.9%

Flight 0.5%

Other Games/ Compilations 2.2%

Arcade 0.5%

Fighting 5.1%

Adventure 5.3%

Role-Playing 5.4%

Strategy 6.2%

Racing 8.4%

Shooter 10.9%

Action 20%

Family Entertainment 19.3%

Sport Games 15.3%

*Percentage of market by units sold

Data taken from The NPD Group / Point-of-Sale Information published by the Entertainment Software Association. "2009 Essential Facts about the Computer and Video Game Industry" http://www.theesa.com/facts/pdfs/ESA_EF_2009.pdf

players] is that women typically spend less time in a single sitting playing than their male counterparts."[32]

To encourage female gaming, new peripherals are being offered, such as pink and baby blue controllers. By making games and the packages they come in more appealing to

Becoming a Video Game Tester

Job Description: Testers are the quality assurance people in the video game industry. It is their responsibility to review games from beginning to end very thoroughly. They make sure that there are no programming bugs or glitches that might cause the game to malfunction. If the game is available on different platforms, such as online, CD-ROM, handheld, or PC, the testers must test each version to make sure each one works the same. They are also expected to make recommendations on how to improve games.

Education: A high school diploma is preferred, and it is easier to get a job with a two- or four-year degree in a computer-related field or other training in computer programming.

Qualifications: Testers should have a thorough familiarity with video games. They should be able to follow instructions well and be very detail oriented.

Additional Information: Testers should not only be familiar with video games, but they should also love to play them. They need to know what the competition is like in the industry so that they can judge whether the games they are testing are unique and cutting edge. They should be excellent at communicating their findings and recommendations for improvements and changes to game designers and other managers.

Salary: about $25,000 to $50,000 per year

young audiences, video game companies hope to keep their customers coming back for more. While this is good for sales, many people think it is not good for the children and teens who play these games.

Encouraging Game Addiction?

In the 2007 Harris Interactive survey, children and teens were asked several questions to help determine whether they were addicted to video games. The participants were asked, for example, whether playing games sometimes seemed more important than doing homework or studying for a test, whether they had ever stolen a game or borrowed or stolen money to buy games, whether they spent a lot of time thinking about games, if they become irritable when they do not play, and whether they use video games to escape from problems in the real world. The participants surveyed were considered "pathological" gamers if they answered "yes" to at least six of these questions, and 8.5 percent of children between the ages of eight and eighteen fell into this category.

Video games can be very seductive. That is, they are designed to draw players in and make them want to play more. For example, in games like *Sonic the Hedgehog* and *Super Mario Brothers,* players earn points or gain strength by overcoming various enemies and obstacles. Players are challenged to complete certain "levels" and then move on to the next, more challenging level.

While the game concepts are fairly simple, the speed of these games can make them challenging and encourages players to improve their skills by playing more often. *Super Mario Brothers,* the first version of which came out in 1985 for the Nintendo Entertainment System (NES), has Mario and his brother, Luigi, fighting mushrooms, turtle creatures, and other "evil" foes in their effort to rescue a princess. It was so innovative and sold so well that many people credit the game

Video game designer Shigeru Miyamoto standing in front of his creation, Mario. The simplicity and speed of games such as Super Mario Brothers *encourage players to improve their skills and play more often.*

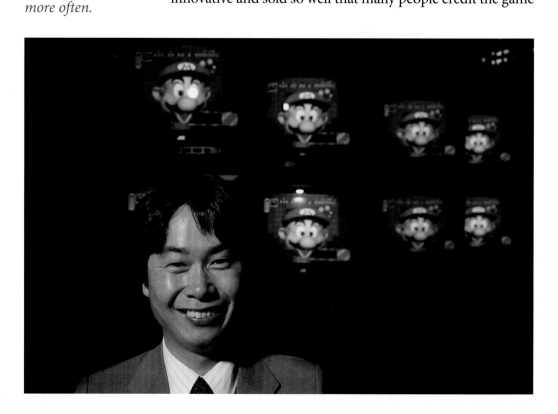

with reviving the industry after the 1983 video game crash.

Sonic the Hedgehog was released in 1991 by Sega for the Genesis system. The improved speed of the 16-bit system allowed the title character—a hedgehog who often rolled up into a ball to gain speed—to move very quickly. It really challenged players' hand-eye coordination and ability to control the game.

As technology advanced, games became more creative, personal, and thus much more captivating. This has been the case, especially, for role-playing games. In role-playing games (or RPGs), players assume the identity of a fictional character who exists in an imaginary world. Unlike earlier games like *Sonic* and *Mario,* these games have an almost unlimited range of possibilities for players to customize their adventures. They can assume their own unique identities, including physical appearance, and really feel as if they are personally interacting with other characters.

Shooter games, such as *Halo,* and other sandbox games also have a fair amount of flexibility. Players can choose to follow a structured game with specific goals, or they can turn this option off and choose their own activities. One of the more recent—and visually stunning—RPG games is *Final Fantasy* (which debuted in 1987 for the NES, newer versions are played on Nintendo's PlayStation or online) and its many sequels, as well as similar fantasy games, such as 1996's the *Legend of Zelda.* As the title implies, it is set in a fantasy world where heroes battle evil monarchs and other wicked forces. Players interact with other characters, some of who are allies, many of who are foes. The animation is of a high quality and encourages players to be a part of a fantasy realm.

RPG games have evolved in recent years into massively multiplayer online role-playing games (MMORPGs). One of the most popular of these is *World of Warcraft,* which is an upgrade of the original RPG called *Warcraft.* Set in a fantasy world of humans, orcs, elves, dwarves, monsters, and other races, *World of Warcraft* is played online and allows people to assume identities, meet friends, form alliances, and create their own adventures.

While these games can certainly be addictive, the increase in online gaming has encouraged more traditional forms of addiction, too, according to some. Among the concerns are online gambling sites and RPGs that contain adult material.

Potential Risks of Video Game Addiction

"Addiction is any pleasurable behavior that renders a person unable to stop once started and which is pursued in spite of negative consequences,"[33] write psychotherapist Hilarie Cash and mental health counselor Kim McDaniel in their book *Video Games and Your Kids*. Addiction to video games is no different than addiction to alcohol, drugs, or gambling. The victims can be children, teens, or adults, and

A worried mother of a video-game-addicted youth visits On-Line Gamers Anonymous for help. Video game addiction is as real as any other addiction that prevents a person from living a well-rounded life.

the consequences are the same. Among the side effects of any addiction is changed social behavior, isolation, conflicts with family members and friends, and an unwillingness to either go to work or school because these activities interfere with playing video games.

Recent research suggests that video games cause changes in the brain similar to the effects of taking drugs. They do this by affecting the pleasure centers of the brain, causing a dependence that is unhealthy. In the view of Cash and McDaniel,

> extrapolating from what is known so far from research, all the popular games exert a tremendously stimulating influence on the brain. Dopamine is being released along with other chemicals, such as cortisol, and adrenaline. . . . There is also evidence that as arousal from gaming increases, some areas of the frontal lobes (the parts of the brain that are responsible for higher mental functions) shut down . . . while other areas of the brain become tremendously active. This means that as arousal . . . increases, judgment and decision-making decrease.[34]

In other words, game-addicted players are less likely to be thinking rationally. They are consumed by a desire to be stimulated by games.

While game addiction can cause video-game players to withdraw from friends and family, another factor leading to social isolation has to do with the player. Many kids, teens, and even adults who suffer from depression or anxiety, hide from the real world by playing video games. Cash and McDaniel think that video games might not cause these problems, but they might contribute to them. They write, "Our experience has been that depressed children seek escape from their feelings, and video gaming offers a very convenient and engrossing escape."[35] Video gaming can also make people with attention-deficit/hyperactivity disorder (ADHD) and Asperger's syndrome (a type of autism that affects a person's social skills) worse. This is because video games encourage social isolation for those who would benefit from interacting with their peers.

Critics of this argument, however, point out that many video games involve two or more players. Everything from racing games where two players operate game controls and race against each other, to complex online games like *Halo,* where players can wear headsets that allow them to talk to each other, form strategies, and cooperate to defeat a common enemy or reach a goal.

Online RPGs Requiring Social Cooperation

Nicolas Ducheneaut and Robert J. Moore, two scientists at the Palo Alto Research Center in California, conducted a study in 2003 that showed how some games really do foster social cooperation. Ducheneaut and Moore studied how players reacted when playing such online games as *Counter Strike, Star Wars Galaxies*, and *EverQuest Online Adventures* (EQOA). They observed people playing the games online for over two hundred hours. They found that many players learned the ropes of the game not by reading instructions but by interacting with more experienced players. The players who knew more about the game proved to be very willing to help the "newbies" understand the game. One of the games, *EQOA,* requires players to cooperate with each other in order to accomplish certain tasks, so players interacted with each other while playing the game. And, during "downtime" moments in games when not much is going on, players socialized with each other by telling jokes or just engaging in small talk.

"There is little doubt that online games have become complex social spaces," concluded Ducheneaut and Moore. They continue,

> Playing a game is about more than mindlessly killing monsters: it is about being socialized in a community, which in turn offers many opportunities for social learning. Through our observations we have begun to show where, when and how players can learn about interpersonal skills in MMORPGs. We argue that many of those skills could usefully translate to the real world, and that games are interesting platforms for players to experiment with interaction techniques.[36]

Athletic Games

The effects of video gaming are not only mental and social, but also physical. As many have pointed out, there is little physical exercise involved in sitting in front of a television or computer screen while clicking away on a keyboard or manipulating a game controller. Ironically, many of the video games that have become the biggest sellers are sport games about football, baseball, basketball, and other athletic competitions. The most successful series in sports video games have been the *John Madden Football* series.

TOP-SELLING GAMES IN THE UNITED STATES, 2008

Rank	Game Title	Units Sold through April 2008*
1	Grand Theft Auto: San Andreas	9.4 million
2	Guitar Hero III: Legends of Rock	8.2 million
3	Madden NFL 07	7.7 million
4	Madden NFL 06	7.7 million
5	Grand Theft Auto: Vice City	7.3 million
6	Halo 2	6.61 million
7	Madden NFL 08	6.6 million
8	Call Of Duty 4: Modern Warfare	6.25 million
9	Grand Theft Auto 3	6.2 million
10	Madden NFL 2005	6.1 million

*Includes games across a variety of platforms – personal computers, video game consoles, and handheld games.

Data taken from NPD Group, published by Forbes.com. http://www.forbes.com/2008/06/03/top-video-games-tech-personal-cx_bc_0603video.html

Sport games have come a long way since *Pong's* debut in the 1970s. Since then, one of the leading companies in video sports has been Electronic Arts (EA). The founder of the company, Trip Hawkins, has been credited with revolutionizing how video games are packaged. He uses appealing covers that are more like those used on music albums to attract buyers.

Hawkins also had the great idea of getting sports stars to sign contracts so that EA could use their names in video games. One of the first such deals was with Julius "Dr. J" Irving of the Philadelphia '76ers and Larry Bird of the Boston Celtics. They signed a contract so that EA could create the basketball game *Dr. J and Larry Bird Go One-on-One*. Released in 1983 for the Commodore 64 and Apple II, the game was a huge hit even though it involved only two players. EA would soon follow it with *John Madden Football* and other games that would license famous sports figures' names.

Today sports games are so incredibly realistic that it is almost like watching real players in a video that gamers can control. They have become so fun to play that people compete in video games rather than participate in actual sports. Of course, television has contributed greatly to the "couch potato" problem, but video game sports have added another distraction from physical activity.

Do Video Games Contribute to Obesity?

Like TV, video games have been blamed for American children not getting enough exercise. In the United States, obesity from lack of exercise and it's associated problems, such as diabetes, vitamin D deficiency (from lack of sunlight), and carpal tunnel syndrome (pain and weakness in the hands from working the controls), have become hot issues in the media and among health-care professionals.

There is some debate among professionals about how much video games contribute to the problem of sedentary lifestyles among America's youth. Cash and McDaniel

Video games have been cited as one reason for the rise in obesity rates amongst children in the United States, but studies are inconclusive on the cause and effect of video games and obesity.

admit that obesity in America's children cannot be blamed on video games alone, but they add that:

a recent study showed a relationship between playing video games and obesity. Researchers at the University of Texas at Austin surveyed almost three thousand children from one to twelve years old, recording their habits, and calculating body mass indices [a measurement of body fat]. They found that the children who played video games were more likely to be overweight than children who watched television and didn't play video games. But there is a twist. This study concluded that playing video games *could be a result* of obesity, rather than the other way around.[37]

This conclusion was reached because overweight kids tend to be less active, and one thing they can do when they are sitting around is play video games.

Authors Lawrence Kutner and Cheryl K. Olson, the husband and wife team who founded the Harvard Medical School Center for Mental Health and Media, note that kids and teens who play sport video games in particular are also more likely to play actual sports than those gamers who played other types of games. They found that these more athletic players often studied video game sports to learn new moves and they "used the video games to improve their skills and understanding of the sports they already enjoyed."[38]

Exergaming and the Wii

Because of the continued improvements in computer technology, there are now video games that actually involve a fair amount of physical activity. A console and controller system

A Breakthrough in Gaming Controls

When Nintendo debuted the Wii controller (or Wiimote) in 2006, it was a breakthrough in gaming controls. The Wii uses motion sensors in a way that makes players feel much more a part of the game than traditional controller buttons. Players can move objects and characters on the video game screen simply by moving the remote around; it can detect not only where, but also how fast a person moves the controller.

The Wiimote works by combining three technologies: a gyrometer, an accelerometer, and an infrared sensor. The gyrometer uses gyroscope technology to detect how the remote moves through three-dimensional space; the accelerometer detects the speed at which the Wiimote moves. Finally, the Wiimote relays this information via infrared light to a sensor placed on the bottom of the television, which receives signals just like a standard television remote control.

Some video games, such as Dance Dance Revolution *and* Wii Fit, *pictured, pair exercise with the fun of the video game experience.*

that received a lot of attention for its ability to motivate players is Nintendo's Wii system, which debuted to the public in 2006. The system features a specialized controller that is able to sense the position a player holds it in a three-dimensional space. It also senses how fast the control is moving. This allows a lot of options for sports games ranging from baseball to bowling in which players actually have to move around physically to control objects in the games they are playing.

Wii is not the first game controller to demand some physical effort from gamers. One of the first such games was the Amiga Joyboard, which came out in 1982 for the Atari 2600. It worked sort of like a joystick, except that it rested on the floor and the gamer actually stood on it. The gamer could then work the board by leaning in different directions, and so the concept was perfect for the skiing game *Mogul Maniac*. Amiga also created *Surf's Up* and a Simon Says type of game called *Off Your Rocker* for the Joyboard.

Light Guns

With all the emphasis on guns in video games, one might think that light guns would be more popular than they are. Originally, as far back as the 1930s, arcade games had guns that emitted a beam of light that was then detected by a light-sensitive vacuum tube on a target. When more modern arcade games were created in the 1970s, the target itself emitted light that was detected by the gun control's sensor when the target was pulled.

When home consoles replaced arcade games as the video game option of choice, gun controllers fell to the wayside. They did not make a comeback until the invention of the NES system. More recently, the Wii has made gun controllers much more popular. The Wii detects targets with motion sensors, which calculate the position of the gun compared to the target on the screen.

In the mid-1980s, other systems came out, including *Foot Craz,* which was released in 1987 for the Atari 2600. It had a controller that was a pad with five buttons on it, somewhat similar to *Dance Dance Revolution.* Because *Foot Craz* came out at the end of the popularity of the Atari 2600, it did not sell well.

Around the same time, the Power Pad was released by Nintendo for the NES system. It was a pad that one put down on the floor. It had twelve circles with the numbers one through twelve on them, with the numbers one, two, five, six, nine, and ten colored blue and on the left (for the left foot) and the other numbers on the right and colored red (for the right foot). The pad worked especially well for a variety of track and field video games, as well as an aerobics game called *Dance Aerobics.* In some cases, the Power Pad was also used in conjunction with other controllers. For example, it could be used in combination with the NES console and a light gun to play *Duck Hunt* and *Super Mario Brothers.*

The control board for *Dance Dance Revolution,* unlike the Power Pad and Joyboard, was designed for the arcade venue, although it has since been adapted for the PlayStation, Xbox, Wii, and even an online version. Simulating a lighted stage with arrows on it, the pad detects whether the player is dancing to the rhythm of the music and matching steps correctly. The game offers text messages of encouragement when the dancer performs well, but it registers a loss of energy for missteps, both of which provide motivation to dance with energy and accuracy. For anyone who has played or watched the game, it is clearly quite a workout.

With the development of the Wii system and its hand controller, almost any sport or physical activity can be mimicked by a video game. Nintendo has also marketed Wii as a way for all members of the family, young and old, to play together and share an experience they all enjoy. With games like *Dance Dance Revolution,* today's players might have found a new way to overcome modern sedentary lifestyles. Debra Lieberman, a researcher at the Institute for Social, Behavioral, and Economic Research and a lecturer in the Department of Communication at the University of California, Santa Barbara, states, "There's evidence that dance pad games like *Dance Dance Revolution* are motivating people to exercise in other ways, and Wii games may have that same effect."[39]

Although many video games remain largely sedentary activities where players sit in a chair and operate controls, it appears that the game industry is changing in ways that will offer people more options for exercise. Other fears about video games, such as social isolation and addiction, might also change with time. There might also be a lot people can learn from video games that stimulate the mind.

Video Games as Educational Tools

Parents are not the only ones who notice how much video games take up their children's free time. Educators also see students becoming increasingly distracted by this fun technology, which has even entered the classroom in the form of handheld games. While they worry about games that involve a lot of violence or that simply keep kids and teens from studying or exercise, they are also starting to realize that video games can be useful tools for education.

Some studies indicate that video games may improve hand-eye coordination and spatial skills the same way that playing with toy blocks does for small children. Spatial skills are gained when a developing human brain becomes used to visualizing objects and concepts in three-dimensional space. Spatial skills are necessary in understanding math and the science of engineering.

While one survey of Americans between the ages of ten and nineteen showed that "those who played video games spent 30% less time reading and 34% less time doing homework," one experiment published by *Psychological Science* in 2007, and cited in a *Parenting Science* online article by Gwen Dewar, suggests that "those who played the action video game substantially improved their spatial attention and their capacity for spatial rotation—that is, rotating three dimensional shapes in the mind's eye. Both males and females benefited, but females made greater gains."[40]

Among the other skills that video games can help improve are vocabulary, reading, spelling, typing, observational skills, and problem solving. When it comes to language skills like reading and writing, many competitive video games can help because they require players to type in commands, as well as read and comprehend instructions quickly. Video games help players learn new terms, too, which are often repeated throughout the game. It has long been known that repetition is a powerful teaching tool.

Computer games offer observational skill training because succeeding in video games requires players to be very aware of their environment in order to avoid threats, locate sources to gain points, find secret passageways, and so forth. Finally, it is believed that video games that include logic puzzles to solve or involve forming strategies to overcome obstacles improve problem-solving skills. Whether a player is figuring out how to get Donkey Kong to make his way through a cave, or battling a dragon with the help of allies, such play stimulates the mind.

The Puzzle Game

It has long been suggested that brains, just like muscles, need exercise to stay sharp. Some doctors recommend that elderly patients might prevent or slow the progress of Alzheimer's disease, for example, by doing crossword or jigsaw puzzles. "Sudoku, crosswords and electronic games can all improve your brain's speed and memory,"[41] according to Mark Stibich, a psychologist who specializes in health behavior.

Of course, there are many video games both online and off-line that are traditional crossword, jigsaw, or word games.

The video game Tetris, *developed in 1985, was one of the first games to stimulate the brain's spatial skills.*

Video games offer a lot more to tease and challenge the brain, however, because a single game can offer a wide variety of problem-solving tasks.

Some of the first brain-challenging video games were fairly simple. *Tetris,* which was created by Alexey Pajitnov at the Academy of Sciences of the USSR, came out in 1985. The game involves a variety of puzzle-like pieces that fall down from the top of the screen to the bottom. As the pieces fall, players must spin them around so that they interlock with pieces at the bottom of the screen. As rows of pieces fill up, the rows disappear, but if a row is not filled up, it remains on the screen. If the screen fills up, the game is over.

Tetris is a good example of a game that stimulates the brain's spatial skills. A 1992 research study published in the journal *Brain Research* further concludes that brain efficiency (as measured by changes in glucose metabolism) increases as people play *Tetris* more. "We believe that the decrease in overall brain glucose with practice reflects a more selective use of brain circuitry, reflecting a better-honed cognitive strategy which was formed during the learning process,"[42] the authors of the study concluded.

Many variations of *Tetris* have been published, as well as games with similar strategies, such as *Yoshi* and *Klax*, that involve matching blocks to clear space; matching puzzles, such as *Alchemy* and *Zuma*, in which the player groups identical images together to clear them; hidden-object puzzles like *Minesweeper*, which is bundled with most PCs; obstacle-course games like *Marble Drop*, in which placing each marble in a maze changes the maze every time; and the *Lemmings* series, which was popular in the early 1990s and challenges players to create strategies to prevent little lemmings from jumping off a cliff. The list of puzzle games is almost endless, and their popularity in home console versions, computers, and online prove that video game players love a good mental challenge.

Modding and Cheats

Playing video games often inspires bright young people to create games as well. Many may start of by modding existing video games. Modding—or modifying—games involves actually writing bits of program that add new objects or capabilities to an existing game. For example, a modder might create a new type of weaponry, a new type of enemy to defeat, or even an entire new scenario within a game.

Modding can also involve creating ways to cheat for players to use to win a game. One common way to edit a game is to add new lives to a player so that he or she does not die as quickly—or at all—when fighting opponents; or, perhaps, a modder might make the hero run faster.

Modding can be a fun hobby, but it is also educational because players learn how games and programming work. Some people who modify games can even show their work to potential employers in the video game industry.

Secret Doors, Cheats, and Easter Eggs

In 1978 Atari programmer Warren Robinett was working on upgrading a game called *Adventure* that was originally an all-text computer game by Will Crowther and Don Woods. The game involved navigating mazes, finding weapons, and battling monsters. Robinett had trouble finishing the game until he was inspired by the Beatles' *White Album*. There is a myth about this music album that says if it is played backwards, it reveals that one of the band's members, Paul McCartney, is dead (he is not). Robinett liked the idea of using a difficult-to-find secret in his game.

So, on one of the walls in a room that was itself difficult to locate, Robinett placed a one-pixel dot that was the same color as the wall. If a player managed to discover it, the dot could be turned into a key that would open a secret room with a message. The message was simply "Created by Robinett" in all the colors of the rainbow. It was not until 1980 that a twelve-year-old player found the room, and the story got attention when it appeared in the magazine

Hidden treasures, secret tricks, and various other tidbits are commonly embedded in video games, only to be discovered once a player hits the right buttons in the right order on the game controller.

Electronic Games. The reporters of the article, Joyce Worley, Bill Kunkel, and Arnie Katz, "referred to the room as an 'Easter egg.' The popularity of Robinett's hidden room was also noticed by Atari. In the future, entire games would be built around hidden surprises."[43]

Hidden passages, secretly stored weapons, special combinations of using buttons on controllers, and other tricks have since become common in all types of video games. Today, there are magazines, books, and Web sites dedicated to offering tips and tricks to gamers on how to find Easter eggs, as well as ways to cheat in games. Cheats are ways to make game programs do things they would not usually do. For example, when playing *Grand Theft Auto* on the Xbox, if a player hits the controls Right, R, Up, White, White, Left, Right Trigger, Left Trigger, Right Trigger, Right Trigger, all the traffic signals will turn green on a street and allow the player to drive more quickly without as much fear of car crashes.

Figuring out these cheats is like a puzzle in which players try to crack the secret code. It takes a lot of time, practice, and cleverness to find the codes. Some players take a lot of pride in discovering them and then sharing the information with their fellow players.

Myst

One of the most challenging and sensational puzzle games of all time is *Myst,* created by programmers Rand and Robyn Miller, founders of Cyan Studios in Spokane, Washington. Originally released in 1993 on the Saturn, PlayStation, 3DO, and Jaguar CD systems, it was later adapted to CD-ROM for play on Macintosh computers and PCs. In 2009 an iPhone version—*iMyst*—was also released. However, it was the home computer version that made it such a huge hit, selling about 6 million copies over the course of several years. Adding its sequels, *Riven* (1997),

The puzzle-solving adventure game Myst *was created by Rand Miller, pictured, and his brother Robyn.*

Myst III: Exile (2001), *Myst IV: Revelations* (2004), and *Myst V: End of Ages* (2005), the franchise sold over 12 million copies.

In the game, the player finds himself or herself on a mysterious island that has been abandoned. The player needs to solve a series of puzzles to find clues about this world and a person named Atrus, who has explored several "ages"—or alternate worlds—and leaves hints behind for those who might follow him. The player then uses the clues and solves puzzles to travel to these other ages.

Possibly one of the most intellectual games ever created, *Myst* has no battles or action scenes. There is almost no interaction with other characters, except for Atrus and his two sons, who have been trapped inside books that serve as gateways to other worlds. Therefore, the focus of the game is to use one's brain to figure out what is going on and not be trapped like Atrus and his sons.

Video Games in the Classroom

Teachers have discovered ways to use games like *Myst* in the classroom. In Bristol, England, for example, teacher Tim Rylands won the British Educational Communications and Technology Agency Award by combining *Myst* with class lessons. For example, he asks students to play the game and then write about their experience. The background music in the game has helped his students become inspired to write their own compositions, using instruments and computer sounds. They have also made their own *Myst*-related videos.

Students ages five to twelve at Rylands's school, Chew Magna, have demonstrated significant improvement in national test scores compared to schools where *Myst* was not used in lessons. A BBC News article notes,

> The national average attainment of Level Four literacy levels [reading at a level appropriate for ages eight to

Video games are often used in classrooms to inspire creativity and boost problem-solving abilities.

nine] for that age group is 75%. At Chew Magna, the number attaining Level Four [has] shot up from 76.5% in 2000 to 93% in 2004. What is more convincing is the level of achievement for boys. The national average for Level Four achievement has stayed at 70% between 2000 and 2004. At [Rylands's] school, the figure has gone from 66.7% to a full marks score of 100%.[44]

In the United States, just like in the United Kingdom, video games have also become a teaching tool in many classroom settings. There are a number of reasons for this choice. Teachers reason that video games help students develop creative-thinking and problem-solving abilities. They are also a way for young people to learn independently, because they will willingly sit down in front of a video game and explore what it has to offer.

An article in the journal *Ode* states,

Video games . . . reinforce self-confidence and compel children to focus attention on an activity. Used properly in the classroom, video games have the power to keep students engaged in learning. People may disagree about whether video games should replace textbook learning, but in a society that is becoming more and more digital, it is evident that video games are teaching skills that cannot be experienced in traditional textbooks.[45]

While using video games in the classroom in this manner is fairly new in education, educational games have been around for some time. *The Oregon Trail* was one of the first educational games. First created in the 1970s by Don Rawitsch, Bill Heinemann, and Paul Dillenberger, it began as a text game. It teaches players about American history and how pioneers settled the West. Players had to determine how much and which supplies to take on their trip in a Conestoga wagon from Missouri to Oregon. They had to survive a number of hazards and see if they could make it West in one piece.

Another early game that could be considered educational is *Where in the World Is Carmen Sandiego?* Created by Broderbund Software in 1985 for the Apple II, the game involves a chase around the world to catch a thief. Players who enjoy the game cannot help but learn some geography

Video Games Inspire Creativity

There are many educational activities that can be planned for students that use video games to inspire creativity. Professor David Hutchinson offers applications for video games in a variety of study areas within his book *Playing to Learn: Video Games in the Classroom.* They include:

1. **business:** Students can learn about advertising by using video from a racing game to design a car commercial; the concept of branding can be explored by comparing packaging on a number of video game systems.

2. **writing:** Students can use an adventure game as the basis to write their own adventure story; they can write a review of a video game instruction book, write dialogue for video game characters, or compose a game strategy guide.

3. **mechanical engineering:** Students can design race tracks, roller coasters, or cars of the future.

4. **social engineering:** Students can design a kid-friendly city based on cities portrayed in games.

5. **social issues:** Students can talk about the problem of bullying, as seen in the game *Bully,* or the problem of body image as seen in a variety of video adventure and fantasy games that portray women as sexually seductive.

6. **the arts:** Students can write reviews of video game music or write a discography of music by a video game composer; they can create their own sound effects, or design a Web site about a video game.

7. **physical fitness:** Students can study health issues, such as poor posture and repetitive stress injuries, caused by playing video games.

8. **math:** Students can gather and analyze statistics on measurable data in video games.

9. **history:** Students can study simulation games, such as *Civilization,* and write their own alternate histories.

10. **geography:** Students can learn about places in the world by locating scenes portrayed in video games on a real world map.

in the process. A series of other geography-related titles as well as detective games challenging other skills followed, such as *Where in Space Is Carmen Sandiego?* (1993), *Where in Time Is Carmen Sandiego?* (1997), *Carmen Sandiego Word Detective* (1997), *Carmen Sandiego Math Detective* (1998), and *Where in the World Is Carmen Sandiego* (2001; a remake of the original 1985 game with the same title).

Today, in addition to using commercially produced video games as educational tools, there are many games designed specifically for class work. Teachers and parents can visit Web sites, such as ABCya! (www.abcya.com) or Vtech (www. vtechkids.com), and find fun games to play that are geared to a particular grade level.

Simulation and Strategy Games

The video game industry has realized that many more mature and experienced players enjoy controlling the course of their games. Teens and adults also like complex games that involve many factors that need to be changed and acted upon by the player. The interest in such games has spurred on innovation in the simulation and strategy game genre.

Sid Meier's *Civilization,* first released as a CD-ROM game in 1991 and later available in other platforms like the Super NES, is considered a classic strategy game that was one of the first of its kind. It challenges players to build an entire civilization beginning with just a few settlers and a small village. There are many factors to consider in the game, including military strategy, choosing what type of government to have, managing food and other resources, developing technology, signing treaties, and keeping the population content so that it does not rebel against its leaders.

Along the way, players can build "wonders of the world," important achievements of society, such as the Hanging Gardens of Babylon, the Manhattan Project, or space flight. Players learn about these historic wonders each time one is built, as well as the history behind scientific advancements. The player wins by either conquering the world or being the first to send a starship to Alpha Centauri. Although at the beginning of the game players choose what type of civilization they wish to be (for example, Aztec, Roman, American, or Russian), it is not until later versions of *Civilization* that this choice really makes a difference. Various civilizations have different strengths and weaknesses programmed into them.

Civilization has become a popular teaching tool in some classrooms, just like *Myst.* "Educational technologist

FOUR STAGES OF VIDEO GAME DEVELOPMENT

❶ Forming a Game Concept

This stage often begins with a brainstorming session to identify the main characteristics of the game. Developers may create a rough sketch or "storyboard" of the whole game, define how the players will interact with it, and write up a concept or proposal paper.

❷ Preproduction

Most often a lead designer or a small team of designers will take the concept further by developing specific characters and environments or "worlds." Artists and programmers work together to create a prototype or a sample version of the game that can be played.

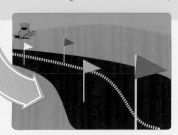

❸ Production

A larger team of programmers, designers, writers, and audio specialists create the intricate details of the game. Characters developed in preproduction are perfected and animated using computer coding. Testing is also performed on early stages of the game, similar to software development; there are versions labeled alpha and beta.

❹ Post Production

This phase includes extensive testing and software patches to repair bugs, game reviews, product marketing and, finally, distribution.

and games-and-learning theorist Kurt Squire has shown that *Civilization* offers students a better understanding of world history, especially the relationship between physical, cultural, and political geography and history," according to video game designer and critic Ian Bogost in his book, *Persuasive Games: The Expressive Power of Videogames*[46]

As is typical in the video game industry, the success of one type of game encourages the release of similar games. *Civilization* inspired other history/strategy games, such as *Age of Empires* (1997), *Europa Universalis* (2000), *Empire Earth* (2001), and their sequels. Other types of simulation/strategy games range from running a business (*M.U.L.E.*, *Zoo Tycoon*, *RollerCoaster Tycoon*), a city (*SimCity*), or even an entire planet (*SimEarth*).

M.U.L.E., produced by Electronic Arts in 1983, is about the economics of running a space colony. The *Tycoon* games have players worrying about all aspects of succeeding in making an amusement park game profitable; there are also a number of other business-related *Tycoon* games, such as *Cruise Ship Tycoon* (2003), *Mall Tycoon 3* (2005), and even *Fast Food Tycoon* (2000). Writing about *SeaWorld Tycoon*, Bogost observed that the business strategies used in the games are familiar to many adults, but they can be highly educational for kids and teens. Bogost writes,

[For] kids, theme parks are sheer magic; the logics by which they operate are deeply hidden, thus the source of their frequent deception. Why, for example, is there a huge toyshop filled with plush seals directly on the (one-way) exit from the seal exhibit?

Avatars

Avatar is actually a Hindi word that refers to the earthly form that a divinity takes. In computer gaming, however, an avatar is an image of a game player's persona or alter ego. That is, it is the appearance of a player as he or she would like to look in a video game. In some online games, such as *Pogo*, people have a limited choice of what their avatars can look like, although they can often customize their hair, skin color, and clothing. More sophisticated games, such as *Second Life,* provide a lot more freedom and individuality. Expert gamers can make their avatars look like just about anyone, or anything, even animals.

Avatars help people to hide behind assumed identities, which is one concern about their use. On the other hand, they also encourage creativity, even artistic and programming skills as players learn how to use the computer to adjust their look and even add animation capabilities.

Why does placing concessions near undervisited exhibits increase their popularity? Who are all the underclass who clean the tanks and the bathrooms so that upper-middle-class youngsters can enjoy their family vacation? Engaging players with these procedural rhetorics exposes the material realities of SeaWorld's operations.[47]

Military Games

While still lots of fun to play, strategy games have introduced some serious and realistic subjects into recreation. One area in which video games are used for serious educational purposes is the military. The U.S. Army and other branches of the military have recognized for years that games like first-person shooters actually are effective and safe ways to train soldiers (the first game used by the military was 1980's *Battlezone,* which was also the first three-dimensional game). The military has been impressed by the realism of first-person shooters,

A soldier demonstrates America's Army, *a realistic computer game that provides civilians with an inside perspective of, and a virtual role in, the U.S. Army.*

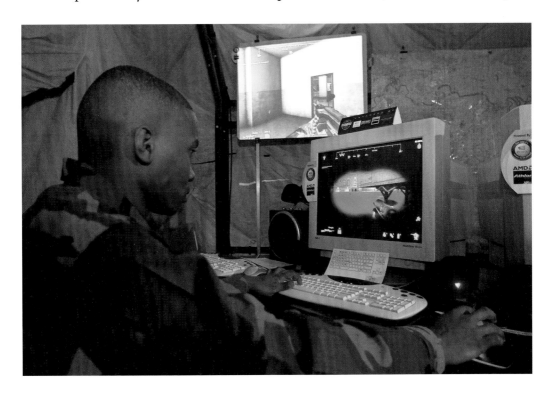

especially games that can be modified by the user to simulate many types of combat situations.

The majority of soldiers entering the military these days are already familiar with gunfights in video games such as *Halo 2*. Training them and presenting new troops to combat theories using video games has been much more effective than lecture classes. "The realism you get is the ability to keep somebody engaged and play a game for three or four hours as opposed to in a classroom, where after 15 minutes they're bored,"[48] says U.S. Navy captain Larry McCracken.

While games like *Halo 2* could prove useful in combat training, the U.S. Army saw an opportunity to do more. Facing difficulties in recruiting soldiers in the late 1990s, Colonel Casey Wardynski came up with the idea of a video game called *America's Army*. This "game"—which was originally released in 2002—is actually an online basic training that over 5 million people have completed. After completing basic training, players then can go on to participate in a variety of mission simulations.

Unlike other shooter games, *America's Army* closely simulates the real army experience, including proper rules of engagement. In other words, players cannot just shoot anyone; they have to follow protocol. Players gain "honor" points for obeying the chain of command, working with fellow soldiers as a member of a team, and performing their duties properly; on the other hand, they can land in jail or be thrown out of the army for misconduct.

Wardynski believes that *America's Army* is an effective recruiting tool, because it shows potential soldiers what basic training and the military are really like. By completing the game successfully, they gain self-confidence that they can do well in the army. "It's designed to give them an inside view on the very fundamentals of being a soldier, and it's also designed to give them a sense of self-efficacy, that they can do it,"[49] says Wardynski.

Games with a Political Purpose

Since America is a land of free speech, it is not surprising that there are also video games that are against war and the military. For example, after the September 11, 2001, terrorist attacks in the United States and the resulting war in Afghanistan, video game developer and researcher Gonzalo Frasca created *Kabul Kaboom*. The game, which is unwinnable, has Kabul citizens being fed hamburgers while avoiding bombs. Ironically, both the food and the bombs are being dropped by Americans, which is meant to be symbolic of the hypocrisy of American policy in Iraq. Other examples of antiwar games are *September 12,* in which the United States attacks Iraq, killing innocent civilians, and *Darfur Is Dying,* which is about the horrors of the refugee experience in Somalia. In this game, war in Somalia results in people losing their homes and becoming refugees, inspiring these ordinary civilians to become terrorists; an endless, unwinnable cycle of violence is produced.

On the other hand, there is also the online game *Kuma\War,* which strives to accurately show current war events and allows the player to take part in them. While other games are designed to show how war causes suffering and often results in more political instability, this game has no real political agenda; it is simply a portrayal of war and violence without any deeper message.

Video games that are against war are not the only politically motivated games. The online community has especially encouraged the release of games with political themes because game designers do not have to worry about costs for marketing, production, and distribution of their software. They can simply post games online.

For example, there are games with environmental-activist themes, such as *Save the Whales* (originally published in 1984 and rereleased in 2002), and games about elections and politicians, such as the *Howard Dean for Iowa Game* and *Take Back Illinois,* which involve election strategy. *Balance of Power,* which was released in 1985, is a strategy game set during the Cold War.

Going beyond individual games, the Games for Change (G4C) community was created in 2004 by over forty foundations and nonprofit groups concerned about the power of games and the Internet to influence society. G4C provides financial and other resources to game designers and companies that wish to create games with a positive social message. *Darfur Is Dying* is one of the G4C games, as well as *Peacemaker,* which is about trying to establish peace in the Middle East, and *Ayiti: The Cost of Life,* which is about raising a family in Haiti.

Video games, in short, have entered almost all aspects of life and human society. They influence people physically, mentally, and socially. They have become more and more realistic, too. The next step in video games has been the blurring of lines between what is real and what is virtual reality.

CHAPTER 5

A New, Virtual Society

After increasing the realism of video game graphics and sound to the point that they are approaching a lifelike quality, the next important advance for video games has been to put control of the game into the players' hands. In the past, designers made all the rules about how a game was to be played, but as players are given more decision-making power, games become more like real life. This is a very powerful evolutionary change in the whole concept of games because it starts to blur the line between what is a game and what is reality.

Traditionally, each game had a specific goal and a specific way to achieve that goal. For example, in arcade games like *Space Invaders* the object was to destroy the aliens before they landed, and the only way to do that was to blast them. Even with games like *Grand Theft Auto* that have sandbox options, there are some limitations for players, such as the characters they can play and the environment of the game.

Today, such limitations have been largely eliminated in video games such as the *Sims* and the online *Second Life*. Actually, these programs offer more than just "games," they are really life simulations. No longer is the issue whether

video games are influencing life. The real question is becoming: are video games *becoming* our life?

The Video Game Community

There is a large community of people out there who love video games, play them often, and associate mostly with fellow players. The Internet is full of chat rooms, message boards, shareware, and game-trading sites to serve people with a passion for video games. These are places where gamers can meet each other and share ideas. There are also plenty of traditional print publications, such as books and magazines, where gamers can connect and share news.

Most of this social networking technology involves simply typing in messages, but now voice communications in real time is possible. Broadband audio connections, which are possible with DSL and cable online services, allow players to talk to each other as they play. Online video cameras can also allow the players to see each other at the same time, although usually players are satisfied with looking at the game screen and hearing each other's voices.

Close friendships have been made between gamers who have communicated with each other in these ways. Role-playing games such as *World of Warcraft* have indulged many people's fantasies of becoming heroic figures and making friends with others who are also playing a role. In other games, such as *Second Life* and *Kaneva*, players might assume a role that is more like their real selves, or they might pretend to have a completely different identity.

Millions of people play online today, living a virtual life where they meet people, have jobs, earn money, buy goods and real estate, go to parties, and much more. Sometimes such activities are contained completely in virtual reality (such as buying and decorating a virtual house), but it is also possible to buy real goods and services through such simulated worlds.

The *Sims*

The game that is really responsible for starting this virtual world phenomenon in gaming is the *Sims*. The first of many *Sims* games debuted in 2000. The game was designed by Will Wright and released by Electronic Arts. Since then, it has become the best-selling video game of all time, selling over 100 million copies as of the spring of 2008. One reason for the *Sims*' success may be that it appeals to both types of gamers: those who like complex action games and "casual gamers," those who enjoy simpler rules of play and are not habitual players. Women, statistics show, tend to be casual gamers, and the *Sims* appeals to this audience. Electronic Arts estimates that 65 percent of *Sims* players are female.

Wright was inspired by the simulation game *SimCity* to create the *Sims* because he

Will Wright, creator of the Sims *video games, programmed the games to give players an unlimited variety of possible scenarios for their* Sims *characters.*

had the idea that a simulated city should be populated by simulated people. Education and learning specialist and consultant Marc Prensky, writing in his book *Don't Bother Me Mom—I'm Learning!*, describes the *Sims* as "essentially a living dollhouse," in which "a player sets up a house, and populates it with people who talk, grow, work, buy, date, mate, have children, and even go to the bathroom. . . . The *Sims* is, in the words of Will Wright, its designer, a huge 'possibility space' in which a player can construct an unlimited variety of possible scenarios, from happy nuclear families, to alternative life styles, to misfits who burn down the neighborhood."[50]

The *Sims* features an artificial intelligence game engine that allows the character to continue its activities even when the player is not controlling it. However, big decisions, such as when to pay bills, eat, or go to the bathroom, are up to the players. Without the player's intervention in these tasks, the character might starve, get kicked out of his or her house, become depressed, or even attack other characters.

Programmers are trying to improve artificial intelligence in games like the *Sims*, so that computer-controlled characters act more naturally and logically, but at this time it is far from being perfected. Meanwhile, the *Sims* was upgraded to the *Sims 2* in 2004, and a third version came out June 2009. The 2004 version contained upgrades such as allowing the *Sims* characters to age more realistically—including the ability to die of old age—and to have more complex psychological needs and motivations. A number of scenario versions of the *Sims* have also been released, such as the *Sims: Vacation* (2004), the *Sims: Hot Date* (2003), the *Sims: Bon Voyage* (2007), and the *Sims: Free Time* (2008).

What Is the Appeal?

When Electronic Arts released the *Sims* back in 2000, they had no idea it would succeed as well as it did. The *Sims* more closely resembles Neopets, which are virtual pets that people have to take care of properly so that they will be healthy and

Artificial Intelligence and Bot Characters

Artificial intelligence (AI) is simply the ability of computers to react to what a game player does. In multiplayer games where some characters are controlled by the computer, the AI characters are called bots or NPCs (nonplayable characters). The goal of AI in computer games is to make these games more compelling and interesting for the player.

AI has gotten steadily more sophisticated over the years. Early games, such as *Pong* and *Spacewar,* did not have AI at all because two players would provide all the input to the computer. As games were created in which a person challenged the computer, however, AI came into play. Computer chess or *Space Invaders* calculate possible responses to a player's moves based on a set of responses limited by the rules of the game (this is known as a hard-coded game). This kind of AI also works in maze, racing, and fighting games.

It was in the 1990s that AI took off with the use of neural network logic in games such as the *Sims* and *Battlecruiser 3000AD.* In these games, bots operate on their own without input from a player and without having to react to a player. Their behaviors are limited, but NPCs can continue to perform actions on their own. Emergent behavior logic came in the twenty-first century with games such as 2001's *Black and White.* Here, the NPCs actually learn to do new things as the game progresses.

happy. In the case of the *Sims,* the players are taking care of human beings instead of cats and dogs.

There seems to be very little excitement in the *Sims,* which mimics the real world of middle-class Americans. Some have wondered, therefore, how the game became so popular. Interestingly the game has been popular as a CD-ROM, but the online version has sold poorly. The reason for this is because players, especially adults, find the *Sims* too personal to share. Rod Humble, head of the *Sims* studio, says:

> What we've discovered is that the *Sims* is a very private experience for a lot of people. . . . It's private because it's set in real life. Rather than on a console in the living room where everyone can see, you generally play on a handheld or on a PC in the study, where no one

can look over your shoulder. You get to tap into this wonderful childhood imaginary game, which is "What if I could create my own little world and all the people in it and watch them go through their business and jump in and change things when I want?" That is a pretty personal fantasy.[51]

Still, for others it is a very dull fantasy. A post on the Absolute Insight Web site tries to explain why the *Sims* appeals to so many people: "You have your working class person who doesn't have much of a life outside of work. It gives him/her a chance to lead a life that perhaps they wish they were leading. It also allows people to design a dream home that they may never be able to own, but still want to enjoy in one way or another."[52] The writer of the post encourages people to do all the activities seen in the *Sims*—such as working, dating, and finding entertainment—in real life. He says, "The *Sims* may be a very popular series with an expansive and lasting appeal for many gamers, but maybe it's time that people think twice about what they are playing before they spend too much time playing it."[53]

The *Sims* and Sexual Relationships

When it comes down to it, however, the appeal of the *Sims* is sexual, according to music and computer games journalist Kieron Gillen. While working for a gaming magazine, Gillen received numerous phone calls in 2000 from people curious about the *Sims*. From these calls, Gillen found that it was not the idea of controlling *Sims* characters as they worked, went to parties, and paid their bills that was appealing to players; there was another common denominator. In an article for the PC gaming Web site, Rock, Paper, Shotgun, Gillen writes,

> There was one similarity about the majority of those phone-calls. After I'd explained the basics, it immediately gravitated towards matters carnal. Can they kiss? Can they have children? Can they have sex? And it's not just the reporters looking for a story—chat to a non-gamer about The *Sims*, and the same questions

Becoming a Video Game Designer

Job Description: A video game designer is responsible for coming up with how a game works from beginning to end. He or she is the head of the project and has to put together and supervise a team of programmers, animators, artists, audio specialists, and testers, who all work together to make the game work. The designer decides how the game will function, what rules the players must obey, what special and fun features will work within the story to make it fun, and how the player will experience the game. A video game designer, in short, is like the director of a movie, managing all the technical aspects and making sure everyone works well together.

Education: A two- or four-year college degree in graphic arts, graphic design, or technical design is preferred, as well as knowledge of computer programming.

Qualifications: Video game designers need to understand current game engines and programming languages, such as C++, Java, and Perl. They should have a good grasp of mathematics and geometry, have good writing skills, good people skills, and think logically in order to plan a strong game. Typically, a video game designer must have several years of experience in game design and development.

Additional Information: A video game designer should be highly imaginative and creative. He or she should be able to conceive of good stories and characters for their video games and appreciate the demands of modern game players. A video game designer also needs to be detail oriented, understand the marketplace and the importance of sales and competition, and work well with other team members.

Salary: $25,000 to $75,000 a year

inevitably arise. It's what they want to know and players are happy enough to tell them. If you listen to people—teenagers especially—talk about The *Sims* . . . the conversation inevitably gravitates towards what one Sim did to another. . . . It is, in some reason, why you do everything else—the point. The pay-off.[54]

Because of the sexual element to the game—especially with the online version—Gillen worried about the potential for online affairs and other misbehavior on the part of players, especially those under eighteen years old. He recommended that the *Sims* be given an age-restriction rating. In addition, sexual relationships within the game should have consequences that are realistic. Gillen says,

> We cannot pretend these things [sexual relationships] do not happen but you can show some of the negative consequences such as families breaking apart, getting pregnant, abortions, and unhappy marriages. These things are taught to us anyway and having them exist in a game would make no difference to our already existing knowledge, in fact it could be quite beneficial to those people who don't see consequences.[55]

Family Bonding Experiences

Animal Crossing, rated E for everyone, is a life-simulation game that appeals to younger players. First released in 2001 for the Nintendo 64 system, *Animal Crossing* is now available online. It features cute cartoon animal characters that, like the *Sims,* go about their daily lives in a charming virtual town. The characters garden, decorate their homes, form friendships, go shopping, and participate in other activities. An interesting feature is that *Animal Crossing* runs on a GameCube internal clock that mimics actual time. So, when it is night in the real world, it is night in the game.

The GameCube version allows four people to play, which, according to video game designer and critic Ian Bogost,

Video games that are appropriate for all ages can encourage family bonding by bringing together younger and older generations for some fun.

encourages families to communicate through the game. Bogost says,

> Since game time is linked to real time, a player can conceptualize the game as a part of his daily life rather than a split out of it. This binding of the real world to the game world creates opportunities for families or friends to collaborate in a way that might be impossible in a simultaneous multiplayer game.[56]

Others also believe that a life simulator game can bring families together. "Families (of all types) live increasingly disjointed lives," commented Henry Jenkins and Kurt Squire in a *Computer Games Magazine* article, "but the whole family can play *Animal Crossing* even if they can rarely all sit down to dinner together.[57]

Capitalism in Life Simulators

One concern that has been raised about life simulators like *Animal Crossing* and the *Sims* is that they may promote consumerism as a means to gain happiness. In *Animal Crossing* there is an emphasis on the players making home improvements, including decorations and building upgrades. Computer characters urge the players to buy things all the time, and soon the gamer is in debt—rather like in the real world. The villain in this story, according to Bogost, is a raccoon character named Tom Nook, who runs the town's store. Nook becomes wealthier as the game progresses.

Bogost noticed that this actually offers a lesson in capitalism to children: "By condensing all of the environment's financial transactions into one flow between the player and Tom Nook, the game proceduralizes the redistribution of wealth in a manner even young children can understand. Tom Nook is a kind of condensation of the corporate bourgeoisie.[58]

The *Sims* games have also been criticized for their focus on money and buying material goods. As game developer and researcher Gonzalo Frasca writes in the journal *Game Studies*,

> one of the most controversial features in the *Sims* is its consumerist ideology. Literally, the amount of virtual friends that you have depends on the amount of goods that you own (obviously, the bigger your house, the

better). Nevertheless, I met some people that firmly believe that the *Sims* is a parody and, therefore, it is actually a critique of consumerism. Personally, I disagree. While the game is definitively cartoonish, I am not able to find satire within it. Certainly, the game may be making fun of suburban Americans, but since it rewards the player every time she buys new stuff, I do not think this could be considered parody.[59]

As life-simulator games transitioned from at-home games to online games, the interactivity of the Internet and the action and graphics of video games merged. This has continued to blur the lines between the two, including in the worlds of business and social relationships.

Second Life

The next advance in video gaming was the creation of a complete virtual world where players can take almost any appearance and indulge in almost any activity imaginable. This was all made possible with the debut in 2003 of the online life-simulator game *Second Life,* the brainchild

The online life-simulator game Second Life *allows players to take almost any appearance and indulge in almost any activity imaginable.*

of Philip Rosedale. Rosedale came up with the idea while studying physics at the University of California, San Diego. After college, he founded Linden Lab in 1999 to help develop *Second Life.*

Rosedale wanted to create a three-dimensional virtual world that closely resembles the real world. Initially he experimented with creating a wearable device called a rig that fit on a player's shoulders and projected the world into his or her field of vision from several computer screens. This way, it would really seem like walking around in the other world.

The rig proved to be too clunky, however, and Rosedale abandoned it. Instead he used just a regular computer screen and online connection. At first, *Second Life* was going to be an online game, with players trying to achieve specific goals. Rosedale soon realized the real potential for a popular virtual community, where players are in complete control of everything within the game.

What makes *Second Life* unique from the *Sims* is this: The *Sims* is a self-contained world where the activities do not affect real life, except for the online version where players can interact; *Second Life,* however, actually has an impact on the real world in several ways. The most notable of these has to d o with economics. In *Second Life* there is a very real economy based on linden dollars. Game players can set up an online account on the site and purchase lindens (a U.S. dollar equals about 270 lindens). They can buy and sell goods to each other and actually run a business and make a product. They can even sell real-life goods and services online. Real estate is a particularly hot property in *Second Life,* with players purchasing land and designing, building, and decorating homes and stores on it, or sometimes renting properties or retail space.

Blurring the Lines Between Reality and the Virtual

A virtual economy brings up a question of how—or if—the *Second Life* economy should be taxed. "Tax law is murky . . .

when it comes to dealings that occur solely within *Second Life* or other computer-simulated environments," remarks CNNMoney.com staff writer Grace Wong. "For instance, is a transaction that occurs only in Linden dollars and doesn't involve any real-world, dollar exchange taxable?"[60] Economic professors are debating the issue. Meanwhile, Wong quotes an IRS agent as saying, "Any time someone wins a tangible prize or award, the value is reportable as taxable income. An accumulation of 'points' would not result in tax consequences, but redeeming or selling them for money, goods, or services would."[61]

Another area where *Second Life* blurs the line between reality and virtual life is how it now functions as a meeting place for businesses, educators, and nonprofit groups. Corporations are using this virtual world to train employees, conduct product demonstrations, and do customer research. Educational institutions as prestigious as Harvard and Princeton Universities have used *Second Life* to hold virtual class sessions, and nonprofit groups have used *Second Life* to hold presentations of their cause, communicate with

Reuben Steiger, CEO of Millions of Us, uses his avatar to transact real world business within the Second Life *game.*

members, and attract and stay in touch with donors.

Perhaps the most bizarre blending of real and virtual worlds is the way *Second Life* has made video games come full circle. Within the game, a player can play video games online. In other words, a person can become a virtual player in an online video game, then enter another virtual world to then play *another* video game.

Inevitably the question comes up as to whether it is healthy for people to immerse themselves in an unreal world. When asked whether *Second Life* is encouraging a physical isolation that can hurt the social skills of young people, *Second Life* creator Philip Rosedale says,

> Whether sitting in front of a computer is bad for you is a function of whether what you are doing there is more or less challenging than real life. If you are mindlessly shooting monsters, the environment has the risk of making you oversimplify the real world. If, on the other hand, you are confronted with a complex human environment with people from all over the world who are demanding of you in your interactions with them, you could actually be better off in front of the computer. *Second Life* can teach people new skills and connect them with new cultures in a way that the real-world environments of many places cannot.[62]

Of course with *Second Life*'s success, many imitators have followed, including the Web sites Kaneva, Entropia Universe, and Active Worlds. Rosedale says a future goal for the *Second Life* universe is to network with other virtual realities. This would create an ever-growing virtual world in which people could play, work, and socialize.

Where Are Video Games Going?

In the 1992 novel *Snow Crash*, author Neal Stephenson portrays a future world where the United States is in decline and

Whether playing an old-fashioned game of Pac-Man *or the most sophisticated virtual reality online game, the world of video games offers something for everyone.*

citizens are withdrawing into a virtual reality world on the Internet. The story revolves around a bizarre narcotic that game players buy in the virtual world but that also causes people in the real world to become addicted. What the real outcome of participating in virtual worlds will be is anyone's guess. Some say virtual worlds, social networking, and gaming are negatively affecting lives and real communities. Some say it is just expanding and changing the human experience.

Business writer and editor Michael Noer predicts that not only will life-simulator games like *Second Life* connect to other life simulators, but they will also network with other types of games. "Going forward, expect multiplayer online games to merge with each other and with social networking sites like Facebook and LinkedIn," Noer writes. "The result will be a virtual meta-universe where your dragon-slaying, 67th-level Paladin from 'World of Warcraft' will be able to seamlessly cross an electronic bridge and end up in a suburban kitchen worrying about the dirty dishes in 'The Sims Online.'"[63]

This virtual gaming world of fantasy and assumed identities may be complicated even more by increasingly sophisticated artificial intelligences. Game characters seen online might be controlled by real people, but they might also be convincingly controlled by a computer program. And, as graphics and animations become amazingly realistic, will the environment of a virtual world look just like our real one? At that point, who will know who or what is real anymore?

Such virtual realities and games may be the trend of the future, but this does not mean that other types of video games will disappear. There will still be a demand for puzzle games, chess, word games, and old-fashioned games where the goal is to gain points, race around a track, or rescue a princess held captive by an angry gorilla.

Chapter 1: Transformation of the Arcade

1. Steven L. Kent, *The Ultimate History of Video Games: From Pong to Pokémon and Beyond—The Story Behind the Craze That Touched Our Lives and Changed the World.* New York: Prima, 2001, p. 16.
2. Steven L. Kent, "Super Mario Nation," *American Heritage*, September 1997, www.americanheritage.com/articles/magazine/ah/1997/5/1997_5_65.shtml.
3. Lisa A. Ennis, "Video Games," in *Dictionary of American History*, vol. 8, 3rd ed., ed. Stanley I. Kutler. New York: Scribner's, 2003, p. 327.
4. Quoted in Benj Edwards, "VC&G Interview: Nolan Bushnell, Founder of Atari," *Vintage Computing & Gaming*, December 12, 2007, www.vintagecomputing.com/index.php/archives/404.
5. Kent, *The Ultimate History of Video Games*, p. 81.
6. Kent, *The Ultimate History of Video Games*, pp. 91–92.
7. "History," Wager Web, www.wagerweb.com/casino/chance-of-glory.cfm, accessed October 21, 2008.
8. Bill Knight, "Pac-Man," in *The Eighties in America*, vol. 2., eds. Milton Berman and Tracy Irons-Georges. Pasadena, CA: Salem, 2008, pp. 743–44.
9. Kent, *The Ultimate History of Video Games*, p. 117.
10. Jason Weesner, "On Game Design: A History of Video Games," Game Career Guide, January 11, 2007, www.gamecareerguide.com/features/327/on_game_design_a_history_of_video_.php?page=4.

Chapter 2: Video Games and Violence

11. Kent, *The Ultimate History of Video Games*, p. 464.
12. Quoted in Lauren Gonzalez, "When Two Tribes Go to War: A History of Video Game Controversy," GameSpot, May 21, 2009, www.gamespot.com/features/6090892/index.html.
13. Quoted in Lawrence Kutner and Cheryl K. Olson, *Grand Theft Childhood: The Surprising Truth About Violent Video Games.* New York: Simon & Schuster, 2008, p. 126.
14. Kutner and Olson, *Grand Theft Childhood*, p. 126.

15. Cherie D. Abbey, ed., *Biography Today: Scientists and Inventors*. Detroit, MI: Omnigraphics, 2003, p. 79.

16. Jake Gilbert, "About Id Software," OldDoom.com, www.olddoom.com/aboutid.htm, accessed October 24, 2008.

17. Quoted in Abbey, *Biography Today*, p. 83.

18. Kent, *The Ultimate History of Video Games*, p. 473.

19. Kent, *The Ultimate History of Video Games*, p. 460.

20. Jose Antonio Vargas, "Shock, Anger over Columbine Video Game," *Washington Post*, May 20, 2006.

21. Quoted in Vargas, "Shock, Anger over Columbine Video Game."

22. Quoted in Vargas, "Shock, Anger over Columbine Video Game."

23. Rashawn Blanchard, "Video Games and Violence: Not Causing Tragedies Since 1971," Associated Content, May 1, 2007, www.associatedcontent.com/article/224962/video_games_and_violence_not_causing.html?page=1&cat=9.

24. Craig A. Anderson and Brad J. Bushman, "Effects of Violent Video Games on Aggressive Behavior, Aggressive Cognition, Aggressive Affect, Physiological Arousal, and Prosocial Behavior: A Meta-Analytic Review of the Scientific Literature," *Psychological Science*, vol. 12, no. 5, September 2001, p. 354.

25. Anderson and Bushman, "Effects of Violent Video Games on Aggressive Behavior, Aggressive Cognition, Aggressive Affect, Physiological Arousal, and Prosocial Behavior," p. 358.

26. Doug Lowenstein, interview, *World News Today*, CNN, May 12, 2000.

27. Quoted in e! Science News, "Video Games and Violence," e! Science News, May 14, 2008, http://esciencenews.com/articles/2008/05/14/video.games.and.violence.

28. Henry Jenkins, "Reality Bytes: Eight Myths about Video Games Debunked," PBS, www.pbs.org/kcts/videogamerevolution/impact/myths.html, accessed October 29, 2008.

Chapter 3: Minds and Bodies at Risk?

29. Quoted in Suzanne Martin, "Video Gaming: General and Pathological Use," *Trends & Tudes*, March 2007, p. 6.

30. Douglas Quenqua, "Survey Finds Women Own More Game Consoles than Men," Online Media Daily, September 24, 2007, www.mediapost.com/publications/index.cfm?fuseaction=Articles.showArticleHomePage&art_aid=67924.

31. Kutner and Olson, *Grand Theft Childhood*, p. 118.

32. Quoted in Walaika Haskins, "Where Are the Video Games Women Really Want?" TechNewsWorld, October 23, 2008, www.technewsworld.com/story/64900.html.

33. Hilarie Cash and Kim McDaniel, *Video Games and Your Kids: How Parents Stay in Control.* Enumclaw, WA: Idylls Press, 2008, p. 16.

34. Cash and McDaniel, *Video Games and Your Kids*, p. 20.

35. Cash and McDaniel, *Video Games and Your Kids*, p. 56.

36. Nicolas Ducheneaut and Robert J. Moore, "Gaining More than Experience Points: Learning Social Behavior in Multiplayer Computer Games," Palo Alto Research Center, www2 .parc.com/csl/members/nicolas/ documents/CHI2004-social_learning .pdf, accessed October 29, 2008.

37. Cash and McDaniel, *Video Games and Your Kids*, pp. 132–33.

38. Kutner and Olson, *Grand Theft Childhood*, p. 216.

39. Quoted in Chinwe Onyekere, "Wii in Action," Pioneering Ideas, February 22, 2007, http://rwjfblogs .typepad.com/pioneer/2007/02/ wii_in_action.html.

Chapter 4: Video Games as Educational Tools

40. Gwen Dewar, "Intelligence in Children: Can We Make Our Kids Smarter?" *Parenting Science,* www .parentingscience.com/intelligence .html, accessed October 30, 2008.

41. Mark Stibich, "Top 10 Ways to Improve Your Brain Fitness," About .com, June 21, 2007, http://longevity .about.com/od/mentalfitness/tp/ Mental_fitness.htm.

42. Richard J. Haier, Benjamin V. Siegel Jr., Andrew MacLachlan, Eric Soderling, Stephen Lottenberg, and Monte S. Buchsbaum, "Regional Glucose Metabolic Changes After Learning a Complex Visuospatial/Motor Task: A Positron Emission Tomographic Study," *Brain Research*, 1992, p. 142.

43. Kent, *The Ultimate History of Video Games*, p. 189.

44. Jo Twist, "Pupils Learn Through Myst Game," BBC News, August 25, 2005, http://news.bbc.co.uk/2/ hi/technology/4160466.stm.

45. Marco Visscher, "Reading, Writing and Playing the Sims," *Ode*, September 2006, www.odemagazine .com/doc/36/reading_writing_ and_playing_the_sims.

46. Ian Bogost, *Persuasive Games: The Expressive Power of Videogames.* Cambridge, MA: MIT Press, 2007, p. 125.

47. Bogost, *Persuasive Games*, p. 181.

48. Quoted in Jamie Holguin, "Uncle Sam Wants Video Games," CBSNews.com, February 8, 2005, www.cbsnews.com/ stories/2005/02/08/eveningnews/ main672455.shtml.

49. Quoted in Josh White, "It's a Video Game, and an Army Recruiter," *Washington Post*, May 27, 2005, www.washingtonpost.com/wp-dyn/ content/article/2005/05/26/ AR2005052601505.html.

Chapter 5: A New, Virtual Society

50. Marc Prensky, *"Don't Bother Me Mom—I'm Learning!"* St. Paul, MN: Paragon House, 2006, p. 72.

51. Quoted in Seth Schiesel, "Exploring Fantasy Life and Finding a $4 Billion Franchise," *New York Times*, April 16, 2008, www.nytimes.com/2008/04/16/arts/television/16sims.html?pagewanted=print.

52. Haggs, "The Sims—Worthwhile or Worthless?" Absolute Insight, April 22, 2004, www.absoluteinsight.net/28.

53. Haggs, "The Sims—Worthwhile or Worthless?"

54. Kieron Gillen, "ErotiSim: Sex and the Sims," Rock, Paper, Shotgun, August 23, 2007, www.rockpapershotgun.com/2007/08/23/erotisim-sex-and-the-sims.

55. Gillen, "ErotiSim: Sex and the Sims."

56. Bogost, *Persuasive Games*, p. 267.

57. Henry Jenkins and Kurt Squire, "Playing Together, Staying Together," *Computer Games Magazine*, April 2003.

58. Bogost, *Persuasive Games*, pp. 269–70.

59. Gonzalo Frasca, "The Sims—Grandmothers Are Cooler than Trolls," *Game Studies*, July 2001, http://gamestudies.org/0101/frasca.

60. Grace Wong, "Second Life's Looming Tax Threat," CNNMoney.com, March 9, 2007, http://money.cnn.com/2007/03/02/technology/sl_taxes/index.htm.

61. Quoted in Wong, "Second Life's Looming Tax Threat."

62. Quoted in Stephen J. Dubner, "Philip Rosedale Answers Your Second Life Questions," *New York Times*, December 13, 2007, http://freakonomics.blogs.nytimes.com/2007/12/13/philip-rosedale-answers-your-second-life-questions.

63. Michael Noer, "The Future of Videogames," Forbes.com, February 11, 2008, www.forbes.com/2008/02/08/future-video-games-tech-future07-cx_mn_de_0211game.html.

GLOSSARY

artificial intelligence (AI): The programming that allows a computer to respond appropriately to input from a game player.

avatar: The appearance of a character used by a player. Usually used in RPGs, avatars can be selected from a predetermined menu in the game or designed by the player.

arcade: Any business venue where video games and other types of games, such as pinball, are played.

bots: Characters in video games that are operated by the computer, not the player.

first-person shooter: A game in which the player views scenes from the perspective of a character whose main goal is to shoot and kill enemy characters.

game engine: The software that is used to operate a video game.

handheld game: Video games with small microprocessors that are compact enough to hold in one's hand.

LCD display: A liquid crystal display system, which is often used for handheld games. Electric current is applied to align the crystals between polarizing filters so that they are either visible or relatively transparent. LCD displays have the disadvantage of being monochromatic—multicolor displays of games are not possible.

MMORPG (massively multiplayer online role-playing games): Multiplayer—usually online—games that allow a vast cast of players to participate.

modding: To modify a game feature, object, scenario, or to create an entirely new game based on a preexisting game.

multiplayer game: Any game that allows two or more people to participate against the computer or against other players.

NPCs (nonplayable characters): Another name for bots.

RPG (role-playing game): Any game in which the player assumes the identity of a character in the game.

sandbox game: A video game that includes a feature where the player can turn off the story line or game goals. The player can then explore the virtual world of the game and sometimes create his or her own adventures.

video game console: A computer system that hooks up to a television set in order to play video games.

Books

Hilarie Cash and Kim McDaniel, *Video Games and Your Kids: How Parents Stay in Control.* Enumclaw, WA: Idylls Press, 2008. Written for parents, this is an easy-to-understand book that explains some of the potential dangers of video games and suggests steps to take to avoid game addiction and other hazards.

Nicholas Croce, *Cool Careers Without College for People Who Love Video Games.* New York: Rosen, 2007. This book describes twelve video-game-related careers, including what is involved in each type of career, what salary might be expected, and what the job outlook is. The book also offers a list of Web sites of industry organizations.

Fred D'Ignazio, *Electronic Games.* New York: Franklin Watts, 1982. Although this book is somewhat dated, it provides a good history of video games, discusses about what makes a successful game, and explores strategies for playing.

Ian Graham, *Usborne Guide to Computer and Video Games.* Tulsa, OK: EDC, 1982. This book may be dated, but it offers a fascinating look into the inner workings of early electronic games. Readers will learn fundamentals, such as how a circuit board works, how video game images are projected onto a screen, and how sounds are generated.

David M. Haugen, ed., *Video Games.* Farmington Hills, MI: Greenhaven Press, 2008. This is a collection of previously published essays debating the pros and cons of video game playing. The book covers health, education, and social issues.

Web Sites

Games for Change (www.gamesforchange.org). This is the Web site of Games for Change, a nonprofit organization that promotes using video games to address social issues such as poverty, human rights, and global warming.

How Stuff Works (www.howstuffworks.com). This Web site offers explanations of how various things work, written in non-technical language. It provides multiple pages on the history and technology of video games and consoles, including multimedia links to demonstrations of the technologies by tech experts.

PBS (www.pbs.org). PBS is a nonprofit organization offering television and online content on a variety of subjects including history, science, and nature. Its Web site offers a multipage section explaining the evolution of the video game industry and the impact of electronic gaming on society today. Visitors can go behind the scenes to discover how video games are made, hear personal gaming stories, and pick up some cheat codes for classic games like *Breakout* and *Pac-Man.*

INDEX

PICTURE CREDITS

Cover illustration: Rokusek Design

© Digital Vision/Alamy, 55

© Interfoto/Alamy, 8

© Keith Morris/Alamy, 9

© RLP Stock Photo/Alamy, 62

AP Images, 9, 36, 39, 41, 45, 50, 57, 66, 73, 79, 88, 90

Gale, Cengage Learning, 32, 46, 53, 71

© Bettmann/Corbis, 8, 23

© Herve Letourneur/Sygma/Corbis, 9

© Ralf-Finn Hestoft/Corbis, 48

© Roger Ressmeyer/Corbis, 18

AFP/Getty Images, 86

Akhtar Hussein/Getty Images, 33

B2M Productions/Riser/Getty Images, 21

Business Wire/Getty Images, 29

Leonard McCombe/Time & Life Pictures/Getty Images, 15

Robert Harding/Getty Images, 11

Sean Gallup/Getty Images, 78

Todd Warshaw/Getty Images, 37

Vivid Images/Taxi/Getty Images, 67

Wallace Kirkland/Time & Life Pictures/Getty Images, 14

Image copyright Leenvdb, 2009. Used under license from Shutterstock.com, 64

Image copyright Steve Reed, 2009. Used under license from Shutterstock.com, 25

Image copyright Jaimie Duplass, 2009. Used under license from Shutterstock.com, 84

ABOUT THE AUTHOR

Kevin Hile is a writer, editor, and Web site designer based in Michigan. A graduate of Adrian College, where he met his wife, Janet, he has been a reference book editor for almost twenty years. Hile is the author of *Animal Rights* (Chelsea House, 2004) and *Little Zoo by the Red Cedar* (Strategic, 2008). He is also the author of *Dams and Levees*, *Ghost Ships*, and *Centaurs* for KidHaven Press, and *César Chávez* and *Cybercrimes* for Lucent Books.